One Faith, Many Faithful

SHORT TAKES ON CONTEMPORARY CATHOLIC CONCERNS

William J. Byron, SJ

D1523083

PAULIST PRESS
New York / Mahwah, NJ

for
Bill Quain, lifelong friend

The Scripture quotations contained herein are from the New Revised Standard Version: Catholic Edition Copyright © 1989 and 1993, by the Division of Christian Education of the National Council of the Churches of Christ in the United States of America. Used by permission. All rights reserved.

All of the essays in this collection, with the exception of "Father Ted Hesburgh" in Part Four, were originally published by Catholic News Service. They have been adapted for this collection by the author, who holds the copyright to them.

Cover image: Courtesy of Shutterstock.com
Cover and book design by Lynn Else

ISBN: 978-0-8091-4759-5

Published by Paulist Press
997 Macarthur Boulevard
Mahwah, New Jersey 07430

www.paulistpress.com

Printed and bound in the
United States of America

Contents

Introduction

This book provides a random access, "thumb-stop" reading experience for those interested in reflecting on the relevance of their Catholic faith to contemporary life.

It is not intended to be read straight through, front to back. Topical in both tone and content, One Faith, Many Faithful is designed to stimulate small-group discussions, conversations between parents and their sons and daughters, and solo flights of quiet reflection for thoughtful people who search for religious significance in the secular happenings they notice all around them.

Since 2001 I've been writing a biweekly, general interest, syndicated column called "Looking Around" for the Catholic News Service. All but one of the essays offered here appeared previously in column format in diocesan newspapers in the United States and elsewhere in the English-speaking world. They've been "road tested" in this way and are arranged here in four parts that reflect the general range of topical coverage. Not all areas of general news coverage are included—no science, for example—simply because my competence is no match for my curiosity at that and many other margins. Nonetheless, the range is fairly broad and the potential for stimulating further reflection through the interpretative framework of the Catholic faith is real.

Principles of Catholic social teaching are explained and applied throughout the book. It is my hope that these pages will assist thoughtful citizens in assimilating these principles and provide motivation to apply them in the practice of faithful citizenship.

WJB

PART ONE

Religion and Ethics

1.

Christmas Is a New Beginning

I like to think of Christmas as a new beginning, and I'd like to use that thought as a way to begin this book.

Christmas was, of course, a new beginning for the whole human race over two thousand years ago, but I wish all Christians would think about it each year as a new beginning for themselves personally, and if enough of them agree and give it a try, this could amount to a major new beginning for all of us all across the world.

The Fourth Gospel, the Gospel of St. John, opens with "In the beginning…": "In the beginning was the Word." *In principio erat verbum* is the Latin version of that message that older readers will remember hearing in what was called the Last Gospel that used to be read at the end of every Mass before the Second Vatican Council introduced liturgical changes in the mid-1960s.

> In the beginning was the Word, and the Word was with God, and the Word was God. He was in the beginning with God. All things came into being through him…. (John 1:1–3)

The "Word," the *Verbum,* refers to Jesus Christ, the Second Person of our triune God—Father, Son, and Holy Spirit. The Divine Word, spoken, as it were, by the Father, is the Christ of Christmas. He was there at the beginning—before time, from all eternity—but not as Christ, rather as the

Word, the creating Word of God. He became Christ at Christmas.

> He was in the world, and the world came into being through him; yet the world did not know him. He came to what was his own, and his own people did not accept him. But to all who received him, who believed in his name, he gave power to become children of God, who were born, not of blood or of the will of the flesh or of the will of man, but of God.
> (John 1:10–13)

St. John is saying that to those who have been born again by faith, power is given to become children of God. We Christians are thus empowered. We are adopted sons and daughters of the triune God. At Christmas, we celebrate the birth of the one who made this happen, who brought this about, who created our world and recreated us.

The best way to make these truths your own in any given year is to think of Christmas as a new beginning for you. There are at least three locations in your life, three areas, where a new beginning might take place: forgiveness; family, and generosity.

Are you at this moment refusing to forgive someone, perhaps even refusing to forgive yourself? Or are you too proud to ask for forgiveness? Forgiveness and apology are first cousins; they live at opposite ends of the same street. If you do think of Christmas as a new beginning, you may have to move up and down that street to attend to forgiveness or apology if you want to experience Christmas peace. What if that street gets crowded? What if Christians around the world begin to think this way?

Peace on earth? Maybe.

The same with family: A new commitment to family love and fidelity, to reverence and respect within the family, can open the door to a very happy Christmas, as can a new approach to the practice of generosity. This doesn't mean giving expensive gifts. It does mean giving more of yourself, particularly your time, without any thought to what's in it for you.

If you practice the virtue of generosity, you will experience the truth of the old saying that "virtue is its own reward." Generosity, with or without Christmas gift wrappings, will surely come back to you.

The possibility of something like that happening all around the world is enough to sell me on the idea that all of us should make an annual effort to turn Christmas into a new beginning wherever we happen to be and thus prepare ourselves for a nice New Year's surprise.

2.

The Principle of Human Dignity

Under the headline "Massacres Shake Uneasy Nigeria," the *Wall Street Journal* ran a front-page story on March 9, 2010, that opened with these words: "The attackers came at night and surrounded this small farming village, firing shots in the air to scare residents from their homes. Men, women and children were hacked with machetes as they rushed out. Several houses were set on fire with residents still inside."

Dogo Nahawa, Nigeria, was the point of origin for this report. It is one of four villages in central Nigeria where members of the predominantly Muslim Fulani ethnic group targeted members of the mostly Christian Berom ethnic group for attack.

Forget the ethnic division. Ignore the geography. Don't even think for the moment about religion. Just focus on the fact that human beings "hacked with machetes" other human beings.

How can this happen in the human community? How can it be prevented? How can every corner of the world be made safe? What is the first step to be taken in any part of the world (including ours) toward a future where hacking and burning—killing innocent others—not only does not happen but is simply unthinkable?

There is a principle that can make all the difference here.

Spelled with an "al," *principal* means main event, top priority, major reason. Spelled with an "le," *principle* means a direction for action, a guiding force, an initiating impulse. Once internalized, principles lead to something. They put "legs" under right values. A principled person knows where he or she stands. Principled behavior is responsible behavior.

The principle that can prevent the massacre described above is the Principle of Human Dignity—a bedrock principle of Catholic social teaching. The church teaches that every human being is created in the image of God and redeemed by Jesus Christ, and therefore is invaluable and worthy of respect as a member of the human family.

Every person—regardless of race, sex, age, national origin, religion, sexual orientation, employment or economic status, health, intelligence, achievement, or any other differentiating characteristic—is worthy of respect. It is not what you do or what you have that gives you a claim on respect; it is simply being human that establishes your dignity. Given that dignity, the human person is, in the Catholic view, never a means to be used, always an end to be honored with respect.

The body of Catholic social teaching opens with the human person, but does not close there. Individuals have a dignity that gives each human person a claim on membership in community ranging from each individual human family all the way out to the world community. Recognition of this claim begins with recognition of the Principle of Human Dignity.

That's where the preventative and protective strategies must begin. Consider the indignities you see all around you. Notice the assaults on human dignity that appear in the form of poverty, hunger, unemployment, violence, disease. Once we start noticing these things, we might begin to address our shared responsibility to explain the Principle of Human Dignity to our young and to incorporate this principle into every aspect of our personal, organizational, national, and international lives.

Once this sort of thinking spreads around the world, machetes will be used only on vegetation and sugar cane, not on human beings.

3.

Understanding the Common Good

The "common good" is a catch-all phrase that describes an environment that is supportive of the development of human potential while safeguarding the community against individual excesses. It looks to the general good, to the good of the many over the interests of the one or very few.

Everyone knows you can't tell a book by its cover. But I have to admit that the title on the cover of a small paperback prompted me to purchase *The Collapse of the Common Good: How America's Lawsuit Culture Undermines Our Freedom* (Ballantine Books, 2002). The author is Philip K. Howard, who gave this book an earlier outing under the title *The Lost Art of Drawing the Line*. The title of another of his books, *The Death of Common Sense* (Grand Central Publishing, 1996), suggests he is preoccupied with the possibility that America is losing its grip on something important. This prompts me to ask in the words of Alfred Lord Tennyson, "Ah! When will all men's good/Be each man's rule, and universal peace/Lie like a shaft of light across the land?" (from the poem "The Golden Year"). Don't look for that to happen soon, Philip Howard would reply. In his view, as expressed in *The Collapse of the Common Good* "any notion of a common purpose is pushed aside by obsession with personal entitlement."

We are losing a sense of working together to achieve common goals and protect the common good. Behind that loss is a reluctance to identify and articulate deeply held values. If, for example, the Principle of Human Dignity is understood, accepted as a value, internalized, and permitted to function as a prompter of personal choice, the person thus prompted will defend human life and dignity wherever and whenever it is under assault. Look around the workplace and the larger community for assaults on human dignity. Try to get behind the unemployment statistics. Look at urban decay. Examine the drug culture and its economic underpinnings. Consider the neglected elderly. Ask about the physical settings within which low-income children seek both education and recreation. How about those who have no health insurance? How do any or all of these social conditions relate to the common good?

In its *Pastoral Constitution on the Church in the Modern World*, the Second Vatican Council (1962–65) described the common good as "the sum total of social conditions which allow people, either as groups or as individuals, to reach their fulfillment more fully and more easily" (No. 26).

Another way—less abstract and far less lofty—of picturing the common good is to imagine it as an automobile tire. If the tire viewed as a whole looks strong, but has a cut, leak, or other point of vulnerability at just one small point, the whole thing will soon collapse. Think of this as the "collapse of the common good"! One, small, unattended point of weakness or vulnerability can lead to the collapse of the whole. In societal terms, it is in the interest of the rich and powerful to assist the poor and powerless; they're all part of the same tire.

We Catholics have to do a better job of understanding the "tire" that is the common good, and then convince ourselves and our elected representatives to do all that must be done to keep our only tire in good repair. We have to evaluate "the sum total of social conditions" in the United States today and encourage our elected officials to do what they can to help all Americans "reach their fulfillment more fully and more easily."

This much is sure: A better understanding of the common good will lead to improved social conditions in the United States and thus to fuller development of human potential.

4.

The Argument for Life

News reports from time to time, along with conversations with friends, encourage me to reflect on the reasons underlying my pro-life convictions. Here's a summary of what typically comes to mind.

I recall a short sentence in a Nov. 24, 2008, Associated Press report on issues that were surfacing then surrounding the upcoming policy debate over whether or not the ban on federal funding for embryonic stem-cell research should be lifted. That sentence accurately portrays the argument against the use of embryonic stem cells as saying "that life begins at conception—that once fertilization occurred in the lab, so did a human being." Hence, no embryo should be destroyed in order to facilitate stem-cell research. I subscribe to that argument, and I admire the verbal precision.

The reference, of course, is to in vitro fertilization. But whether in the womb or in the lab, when fertilization occurs, there is life. This is undeniable. A being exists that did not exist before.

Because it is human life—on its way to becoming fully human—it is, the argument goes, a human being. To assert that it is not human because it is not yet fully human is to deny the reality that a continuum of existence has begun.

This is not to say that the embryo is a human person; it may well be, but that is not the claim. The claim is simply that a being exists that is on its way to becoming fully human. To terminate, for purposes of research, what would otherwise be an inevitable biological development to full human personhood, is morally wrong.

That conclusion can be drawn from human reason without the guidance of divine revelation or the rulings of organized religion. Reason sees in the fertilized egg an incipient human person and concludes that this is a life worthy of respect and protection. Those who disagree and see no human life in this living being at the moment of conception are, in my view, not to be dismissed as having no respect at all for human life and dignity. They are, however, to be confronted on the issues of (1) when human life begins, (2) why any human life should not be regarded as a human being (if something exists, how can it not *be*?), and (3) why a developing human being has no claim on the possession of actual or potential personhood.

To engage in a verbally imprecise policy debate about embryonic versus adult stem-cell research would be to walk mindlessly past the possibility of widespread violation of human life, human rights, and human dignity. I would compare this to firing a rifle through a closed door when there is a possibility that a person is standing there on the other side.

We, as a nation, are not very good at engaging in verbally precise, reasoned argument on the life issues. The chances of that happening will improve, I think, if we show more respect for one another and permit ourselves to engage in respectful moral argument.

New forums may have to be found to facilitate this exchange. Whether the forum is a two-way conversation, a legislative debate, a group discussion, or a university seminar, the human hearts and minds that shape and debate the arguments will, I would hope, recognize that each share one thing in common: They all possess a human life that began at the moment of conception. If they can't agree on that, you have to wonder where—if anywhere—the conversation can begin.

But begin it must. And we Catholics have a special responsibility, I believe, to approach this issue in Christ-like fashion, in a clear, persuasive argument, not in a coercive, threatening manner, and certainly in an altogether nonviolent way. In this regard, we might well consider the example of Mahatma Gandhi and his understanding of the essence of the principle of nonviolence, namely,

> "...that it must have its root in love. Its object should not be to punish the opponent or to inflict injury upon him. Even while non-cooperating with him, we must make him feel that in us he has a friend and we should try to reach his heart by rendering him humanitarian service wherever possible." (quoted by Eknath Easwaran in *Gandhi the Man: The Story of His Transformation*, Nilgiri Press, 1997)

This is the way Gandhi confronted power; this is the way Gandhi led. This is an approach we should consider taking when we venture into the public policy arena to make our case against abortion.

We have a great tradition of Catholic social teaching that rests on a bedrock principle of the Dignity of the Human Person. Respect for human life is another basic principle in that great tradition. Catholic social teaching views human life at every stage of development *and decline* as precious and therefore worthy of protection and respect. Although moral arguments about abortion, capital punishment, euthanasia, and the use of nuclear weapons tend to dominate ethical discourse on the life issues, it is important to remember that this nation, indeed all nations, deal with a broad range of life issues all the time. Think, for instance, of matters of concern to business and professional people in America every day: consumer product safety; pharmaceutical research and marketing; occupational health, mine safety, and other workplace safety considerations and of food production: preparation, packaging, and marketing. Examine a list of federal regulatory agencies and you have the makings of an agenda for a review of ethical concerns relating to human life that conscientious producers and consumers have always to keep in mind.

The right to life and our corresponding concern for the protection of life reach far beyond medical ethics to include issues that we often fail to recognize as human life issues at all. This is not to dismiss or in any way dilute our medical ethical concerns; they are essential. But they will be more readily recognized and respected to the extent that we are successful in promoting a culture of life, a broadly shared commitment in a set of shared meanings and pro-life values that are clearly articulated and rooted in a recognition of the dignity of the human person and the value of human life.

As Gandhi stated so well in the passage above, our position "must have its root in love." It should not be about punishing our opponents or inflicting injury upon them. We must treat those we disagree with as friends and try to reach their hearts by "rendering [them] humanitarian service wherever possible."

I think Jesus would agree. He would, I think, encourage us to make our pro-life case clearly, gently, persuasively, and from the heart.

5.

Social Justice and the Environment

"If you want to cultivate peace, protect creation," wrote Pope Benedict XVI is his January 1, 2010, World Peace Day message.

This echoed the January 1, 1972, World Peace Day statement of Pope Paul VI: "If you want peace, work for justice." Paul VI made a related point in his 1967 encyclical *Populorum Progressio* ("On the Development of Peoples") when he remarked that "development is the new word for peace."

Papal social teaching says that if we work to protect the environment, we are preparing the way for peace. If we work for justice, peace will eventually follow. Economic development is prerequisite to the attainment of world peace.

This is clear and consistent Catholic social teaching. Pope Benedict's concern for the environment ("protect creation") is part of a worldwide concern that marks the confluence of two great social forces: the social justice movement and the environmental movement.

I was struck by a comment made by former President Bill Clinton in his eulogy at the funeral of Smith Bagley, who died in early January 2010. Mr. Bagley was a philanthropist, a convert to Catholicism, a Democratic Party fund raiser, and supporter of social programs to improve the lot of poor and disadvantaged people. Mr. Clinton said, "References have been made several times today to the fact that Smith was a convert to Catholicism. I'd say that Smith was a Catholic before he ever became one, because of his social conscience and his commitment to social justice."

And that made me think of something former British Prime Minister Tony Blair said in a talk given to the National Leadership Roundtable on Church Management in that same year at the Wharton School of Business at the University of Pennsylvania. Blair spoke, among other things, of his own conversion to Catholicism and first remarked that you would have to be British to understand why he could never had made that move while still prime minister. But after leaving office he did make the move.

> One of the reasons I was drawn to the Church was the work that it does caring for the sick, looking after the elderly, and showing compassion for people for whom most people don't show compassion....I know the help that our Church gives in the work that is done in some of the poorest parts of Africa in pursuit of justice, and indeed life for people who otherwise are going to die as a result of famine or conflict or disease.

Catholics can take pride in this respect for the Catholic commitment to protect the poor and promote social justice. But Catholics have to realize that their great tradition of social justice is at risk if it fails to connect in the policy arena worldwide with the great social issues of our day: climate change, poverty, unemployment, economic development, hunger, disease, the life issues, refugee movements, family instability, education, and many more.

If we want peace (and who doesn't?), we must deal with all these issues. Pope Benedict seems to think that environmental protection would be a good place to start. Take an intellectual or practical walk down that path and you will meet all the other issues along the way. "It is becoming more and more evident," said Benedict in his 2010 New Year's Day message, "that the issue of environmental degradation challenges us to examine our life-style and the prevailing models of consumption and production....We can no longer do without a real change of outlook which will result in new life-styles."

6.

Road Map for a "Journey of Hope"

Pope Benedict XVI was speaking to about 25,000 seminarians and young people on the next-to-last day of his 2008 six-day visit to the United States when he said, "walking in the Lord's footsteps, our own lives become a journey of hope." He might just as well have had all Christians in mind as he mapped out this path of discipleship.

He began by recalling that Saint Peter urged all Christians to "proclaim the Lord Christ" and to "always be ready to make your defense to anyone who demands from you an account of the hope that is in you" (1 Pet 3:15). So this successor of Peter took the occasion to repeat Saint Peter's challenge and "share with you some thoughts about being disciples of Jesus Christ." Benedict described discipleship as "walking in the Lord's footsteps." Take that walk, he said, and your life becomes "a journey of hope."

Twice in the talk, Benedict urged his listeners to offer "an outstretched hand of hope" to those they meet along the way and by that simple gesture perhaps "awakening in them a life of faith." After recalling that his own teenage years "were marred by a sinister regime" (Nazism in Germany) that was eventually "recognized for the monster it was," he went on to say that the "power to destroy...never triumphs." We recall this most dramatically, he said, in the season of Easter and he noted that the conviction that the power to destroy never triumphs "is the essence of the hope that defines us as Christians."

Unbelievers have first to see some signs of hope before they will be prompted to ask, as Saint Peter said they would, about "an accounting for the hope that is within you." By making the "hand of hope" visible in our time, we Christians can, in Pope Benedict's view, help to dispel the darkness of heart and mind in our world.

That darkness sets in, he said, "when people, especially the most vulnerable, encounter a clenched fist of repression or manipulation rather than a hand of hope." He had in mind those "affected by drug and substance abuse, homelessness and poverty, racism, violence, and degradation— especially of girls and women." Acknowledging that the causes of these problems are "complex," Pope Benedict said they are rooted in "a poisoned attitude of mind" and a certain "callousness of heart." "Such tragedies also point to what might have been and what could be, were there other hands—your hands—reaching out."

"We are tempted to close in on ourselves, to doubt the strength of Christ's radiance, to limit the horizon of hope. Take courage! ...Let your imaginations soar freely along the limitless expanse of the horizons of Christian discipleship." And then he outlined a road map for discipleship by calling attention to "four essential aspects of the treasure of our faith: personal prayer and silence, liturgical prayer, charity in action, and vocations."

In personal prayer and silence you can hear God's call, he said. You can "look about you with Christ's eyes, listen with his ears, feel and think with his heart and mind." Out of this prayer "hope in action" can emerge. Putting it bluntly, Pope Benedict asked the young: "Are you ready to give all as he did for truth and justice?"

Liturgical prayer brings you "closer to God and also prepares you to serve others," prepares you for "charity in action." When he turned to vocations, Benedict first praised "the vocation of marriage and family life," and then urged consideration of the call to priesthood and religious life. In responding to your call, he said, "Remember that what counts before the Lord is to dwell in his love and to make his love shine forth for others."

7.

Two Interesting Signs of the Times

In 2009, several news stories crossed my desk around the same time. Their headlines proclaimed interesting signs of the times in the life of the Catholic Church in the United States.

First, this headline on a Catholic News Service release: "Former Pittsburgh Catholic Church Being Converted into Mausoleum." Then I saw a *New York Times* headline about a plan by Mayor Bloomberg to turn closing Catholic schools into charter schools, and another *Times* story in which Bloomberg was described by a New York bishop as Noah with a life preserver.

Mausoleum? Life preserver? Death and rescue-from-death make interesting news at any time, but applied to institutions of the Church, they raise signs that should be read carefully by religious believers who should know that, although they cannot predict the future, they can chose the future they want to have. Become the change you want to see occur, said Gandhi. Become the leaders you say your country needs, I tell my students in a college classroom course on leadership.

I'm intrigued by the mausoleum image. It is so heavy, grim, gray, and immobile. It is just the opposite of the image Jesus conveyed to those who would follow him. He launched a movement. Sadly, many who think of themselves as his followers have permitted the movement to become a monument. Institutional immobility, unmarketable real estate, obsolete rectories, empty convents, excess classroom capacity, not to mention ceremonial trappings and honorific titles are making us irrelevant in cities and towns that desperately need what the Church has to offer. Weighed down with the physical, we are impeded in our spiritual, liturgical, and apostolic outreach.

The Pittsburgh mausoleum, the former St. Mary Church in Lawrenceville, is serving an admirable purpose—providing "880 crypts and 712 niches for cremated remains along the interior walls, plus a commitment chapel in the former sanctuary with seating for up to 200 people." It is also providing, for those who have eyes to see, an image that serves as a reminder that there is need for creative, imaginative, pastoral leadership to guide the "movement" of word and sacrament toward those who need it, especially the young.

Then we have the image of "Noah with a life preserver": Mayor Michael Bloomberg of New York City. He can, according to the Times, "convert four Roman Catholic schools singled out for closing into public charter schools, an 11th hour lifeline meant to preserve the education provided in the buildings and stave off potential overcrowding in city schools" It was Brooklyn Bishop Nicholas A. DiMarzio who, in unveiling the plan with Mayor Bloomberg at a city hall news conference, recalled the story of Noah's ark. He referred to the "flood situation" facing the church financially. He compared the mayor to Noah and said: "He's throwing out a life preserver and I'm going to grab it" (Javier C Hernandez, "Mayor and Bishop Propose a Plan to Save Schools," *New York Times*, February 7, 2009).

The city would lease the buildings from the diocese. There would be no religious instruction or religious symbols in the newly constituted charter schools. There are legal, political, and educational hurdles to be cleared as the negotiations between the diocese and the city proceed. There is also a lot of planning to be done by the diocese as it looks ahead. A generous supporter of Catholic education in Baltimore once remarked to me, "It wasn't raining when Noah built the ark." More rain will surely fall over Catholic institutions. More thought has to be given to the design and construction of new arks to keep us afloat. And you'll find further reflection on this issue in Part Three of this book.

8.

Don't Call It Marriage

An amendment to the Defense Authorization Act for fiscal year 2010 added acts of violence against gay, lesbian, bisexual, and transgender persons to the list of federal hate crimes. President Barack Obama signed it into law on October 28, 2009. It's the first major piece of federal legislation in support of the rights of homosexuals and is being compared with the passage of 1960s civil rights legislation that empowered countless African Americans.

This law acknowledges the dignity of persons regardless of their sexual orientation and is a development to be welcomed by all who are committed to the principles of justice and human dignity.

News of the passage of this legislation triggered expressions of hope from gay-rights activists that additional federal legislation would soon be passed to protect homosexuals from workplace discrimination, admit them to military service, and recognize their right to same-sex marriages. A year later, in December 2010, Congress repealed the military's "don't-ask-don't-tell" policy that prohibits openly gay men and women from enlisting or remaining in military service. And it is likely that federal legislation barring employers from firing employees on the basis of their sexual orientation will soon become law.

The third issue—federal recognition of same-sex unions and calling those unions marriage—will be defended by proponents as an antidiscrimination issue, but draw opposition from the Catholic community, which sees not discrimination, but defense of marriage—a sacramental union between a man and a woman—as the issue. In the Catholic understanding, bride (female) and groom (male) confer that sacrament on one another; the priest or deacon is simply the official witness. There is no room for a same-sex union in the Catholic understanding of marriage.

Catholic opposition to same-sex marriage will be more persuasive to the extent that it is explained by spokespersons who are unambiguous in their support of protection by the state of the rights of homosexuals in the matter of hate crimes, workplace discrimination, and military service. The Catholic commitment to justice should also support partners in a same-sex union having, as a spouse would have, inheritance rights and access to a partner's hospital bedside in times of illness.

Permitting partners in a same-sex union to have adoption rights is another matter. Here Catholic opposition should be grounded in sound theory and solid data, evidence that the arrangement would not be good for children. It should rest on discretionary, not discriminatory, grounds and in no way impugn the dignity of any homosexual person.

The Church has the ongoing challenge of defending its distinction between homosexual orientation (morally neutral) and homosexual behavior (morally impermissible). Pastoral explanation of this distinction remains a challenge for the Church, which is not to say that it cannot be met.

Marriage, in the eyes of the Church, is a sacrament. If the separation of Church and state means anything, it certainly means that the state is not free to decide what is and what is not a sacrament, even though the state and other civic jurisdictions do, without objection from the Church, issue what are called marriage licenses.

If the state decides to approve and protect same-sex unions, the Church will insist that the state has no right to call these unions marriage. The long-standing acceptance of marriage licenses issued by the state poses a difficulty for the Church in making that argument. Without yielding any moral ground, however, the Church can accept a two-tier system, common in other countries, of having Catholics appear before a civil authority in a civil ceremony to be followed by a church ceremony where the sacrament in conferred. Other religions may, if they wish, welcome partners in a civilly recognized same-sex union to a subsequent religious ceremony of commitment. Some denominations will surely do that; the Catholic Church will not. Its refusal to do so must be respected as an expression of commitment to sacramental marriage, not a condemnation of those with other views.

9.
_____

More on the Same-Sex Marriage Debate

A federal judge in California ruled in 2010 that Proposition 8—that state's 2008 ban on same-sex marriages—amounts to unfair discrimination against gays and lesbians and therefore violates the U.S. Constitution. To no one's surprise, the Church, which supported Proposition 8 when it was a referendum issue being debated several years earlier, disagrees with this decision and will work for reversal as this case moves through various stages of appeal on its way, most probably, to the U.S. Supreme Court.

I've read the 135-page decision of Federal District Court Judge Vaughan Walker. It states: "Because Proposition 8 disadvantages gays and lesbians without any rational justification, Proposition 8 violates the Equal Protection Clause of the Fourteenth Amendment [to the U.S. Constitution]." Judge Walker concluded: "Proposition 8 fails to advance any rational basis in singling out gay men and lesbians for denial of a marriage license. Indeed…Proposition 8 does nothing more than enshrine in the California Constitution the notion that opposite-sex couples are superior to same-sex couples."

The *New York Times* (August 4, 2010) welcomed Judge Walker's decision editorially as "a stirring and eloquently reasoned denunciation of all forms of irrational discrimination." The Church, of course, is also opposed to discrimination. So the question now seems to come down not only to whether any form of rational discrimination might be acceptable, but what, in fact, is discrimination? How does discrimination differ from prejudice? And when might ordinary human discretion be acceptable, even desirable, even though it necessarily involves denial or exclusion?

The Church will say that it has a rational justification for its stand against same-sex marriage. It holds that marriage is a sacrament, a sacred bond that can be established only between a man and a woman because it has a procreative purpose as well as the purpose of enabling two human beings to become more fully human in the expression of their love for one another. Bride and groom confer the sacrament on each other. The Church recognizes and blesses this bond.

Opposition to same-sex marriage is not a matter of the Church wanting to legislate morality, even though it does teach that homosexual acts (as opposed to orientation) are immoral. Nor is this an instance of the Church declaring that homosexual persons are somehow inferior to or less than equal to heterosexual persons, as Judge Walker asserts.

In order to be credible and convincing in arguing that equality is not served by redefining marriage to accommodate same-sex couples, the Church must be unambiguously supportive of the full range of human, economic, political, and civil rights for gays and lesbians.

In order to mount an effective defense of marriage in the public policy arena where it has every right to make its convictions known, the Church may have to a accept state-approved (licensed) domestic partnerships—same-sex unions—as a way of protecting homosexual persons from unfair discrimination in employment, health-care, inheritance, and ownership issues. Domestic partnerships are already protected by law in California but, in the judgment of Judge Walker, that falls short of equal protection under the law.

On a related matter, the Church will have to rely on the strength of the best social science data to inform its decisions on the question of granting or refusing adoption rights to same-sex couples.

And in the absence of any biological discovery of a "gay gene," the Church will have to exercise compassion and pastoral sensitivity in dealing with the "this is the way God made me" argument that is not going to go away.

None of this debate is going to go away any time soon.

10.

Facing Up to the Clergy Sex-Abuse Scandal

Holy Week was more solemn and serious in 2010 for many Catholics due to public disclosure of allegations of clergy sex abuse of children in Ireland, Germany, the Netherlands, Austria, and Switzerland. Catholics worldwide were shaken by criticism of Pope Benedict XVI. Concern for the victims was on our minds. The search for reasons, which began in the United States eight years earlier, was reopened. How, we found ourselves asking, can the church make amends and what must be done to prevent a recurrence ever again?

For me, the path of analysis begins at the entry gate—two gates, really. The first is the threshold one crosses when entering a seminary; the second is advancement to orders.

If I were a bishop or admitting provincial, I would want to know the sexual history of every candidate. This is extraordinarily intrusive, I know, and invasive of privacy. No one would be forced, however, to continue, or even to begin to participate in this conversation, but the conversation between the candidate and the admitting authority to a sem-inary should, I believe, touch on the delicate questions of how one has managed his sexuality, on whether one's sexual identity is adequately known to himself, and whether one feels truly called to and capable of meeting a commitment to celibacy.

If the candidate had been sexually abused as a child, that fact should be known. Not that it would of itself be dis-qualifying, but it would open up an honest examination of whether or not the psychological impact of the violation has been dealt with so that the probability of the victim ever becoming a violator would be judged to be minimal. Exceptional care would have to be taken to avoid creating the impression (or aggravating an impression already there) that the young man caused the abuse or is morally responsible for it. Any victim of abuse as a child must be a psychologically healthy young adult when entering the seminary. On this point, I would say that serious doubt should be disqualifying.

Similarly, when it is time to advance a seminarian to orders, the same kind of special, even sacred conversation should take place. If the commitment to celibacy has proved to be unmanageable, if anything even remotely resembling the criminal behavior that produced the scandals we all now deplore occurred during the seminary years, the candidate should be denied admission to orders.

As harsh as these steps appear when laid out here in cold print, it would be wise for bishops, superiors, and seminary rectors to apply them now retroactively and confidentially to those famous files that have been turned over, however belatedly, to criminal prosecutors. What if these procedures had been in place many years ago when the tragic figures now called cases sought admission to the seminary or requested advancement to ordination? Could some cases of subsequent abuse have been prevented? If, as we say perhaps too glibly when we talk about cases of clergy sexual misconduct, "even one is too many," would it not follow that application of a guideline that would bar advancement to ordination would have served the interest of protecting children?

Conversations along these lines are now happening in many dioceses and religious orders around the world. This is an obvious preventive measure. It is also a welcoming, encouraging, and positive assist on the part of those in authority to healthy young men of generosity and talent, whom God is calling to ordained ministry. We can only hope and pray that they will not be discouraged by reports of past failures in the wounded Church they want to serve.

11.

The Celibate: A Crowd of One

Whatever the controversy over priestly celibacy in the Church these days, care must be taken not to lose appreciation for the way the celibate participates in the mystery of the grain of wheat. "Very truly, I tell you, unless a grain of wheat falls into the earth and dies, it remains just a single grain; but if it dies, it bears much fruit" (John 12:24). A comparison with the mystery of the wheat grain suggests that the "death" of celibacy can bring forth life; it can "produce much fruit."

That celibacy can be fruitful is an overlooked consideration in the turmoil surrounding priesthood today. I'm convinced that there can be reproduction in the order of grace through celibacy. This is a misunderstood and often neglected dimension of priestly existence. Faith is needed to see it and believe.

Many people, even many priests, view celibacy as baggage to be lugged through life on the journey of priestly service. Some see it as purely functional—freeing a person up for ministerial service. Times change, and what once was functional can become a hindrance. So there is talk about optional celibacy for diocesan or "secular" priests, as was in fact the case for centuries in the life of the Church. That option may someday be once again available in diocesan priesthood.

Should celibacy be optional for the order or "religious" priests as well—the Benedictines, Franciscans, Dominicans,

Jesuits, and other communities whose members take the vows of poverty, chastity, and obedience? Celibacy is one of the organizing principles for religious community life where members commit themselves to live with the empty purse of poverty, the empty arms of celibacy, and the emptying out of self-will in obedience to superiors. This they do in imitation of the poor, chaste, and obedient Christ.

Those who live religious life will be the first to assure you that these conditions involve sacrifice but not at the price of personal diminishment. The vows, including celibacy, are one way of participating in the mystery of the grain of wheat.

All analogies limp, of course, but here's one that gets along without a crutch and can help open minds wrap themselves around the rationale for celibacy. You walk into a room at night and flip a switch on the wall. Lights come on, but you rarely give a thought to the source of the illumination. There is a power generator somewhere unknown to you, providing the light.

I firmly believe that celibacy, in God's gracious providence, is one of many sources—another would be human illness—that generate power for others in the order of grace. It generates grace to overcome difficulties, to bear illness, to resist temptation. I'm convinced that there is reproduction—production of new life—in the order of grace because of dedicated priests living celibate lives today. This applies not just to religious priests, but also to those who have answered the call to celibacy in diocesan priesthood. The Church they serve may someday offer the call of optional celibacy to their successors in the ranks of diocesan priesthood. Who can say? If that option does in fact emerge, God may still continue to call some men to celibacy in the diocesan priesthood. The call to celibacy is a gift that will continue to be offered in the Church to men and women, lay and religious, ordained and nonordained, so long as God wills it to be.

The celibate, I believe, is a crowd of one doing more good in this world than any of the worldly wise could ever begin to imagine.

12.

Considering "the Alternative"

I have a friend who typically conveys news of someone's death by remarking that the deceased person "has joined the majority." Another friend likes to say, "He rolled a seven," when reporting that someone we both knew has died.

Deaths of celebrities like Michael Jackson, Farrah Fawcett, and Ed McMahon, within days of each other several years ago, had the effect of forcing people to think about, if not face up to, the inevitability of their own deaths. Few of us are famous for doing that, although we read about the deaths of celebrities every day.

I spoke to a woman not long ago who was well on the road to recovery after a serious illness and she said, "I'm doing just fine now, considering the alternative." "But did you ever really consider the alternative?" I asked. She smiled and said, "I guess I should." So should we all.

"But, as it is written, 'What no eye has seen, nor ear heard, nor the human heart conceived, what God has prepared for those who love him'" (1 Cor 2:9). Those words are part of divine revelation. That's God speaking to each one of us. But we refuse to listen in faith. We refuse to permit ourselves positively and hopefully to consider "the alternative."

In an interesting book, *Life, Death, and Christian Hope* (Paulist Press, 2009), Daneen Georgy Warner reflects on the meaning of hope in the context of death. She points out that because they fail to see their own death in the light of Christ's death and resurrection, many Christians "place their faith and hope in medicine" and thus "harbor a false sense of security concerning their mortality."

If you really believe in the resurrection of Christ, death is behind you. "Death's not what you're moving toward," as the African-American priest-liturgist Father Clarence Rivers put it many years ago, "it's what you're coming from!" The challenge for us, as Daneen Warner explains, is to face up to our cultural bias against accepting the fact that death is an inevitable part of life, by "shifting our hope in human powers to hope in God." That means taking it on faith that the death and resurrection of Jesus have overcome death for all who believe in Jesus.

Have the courage now to think out loud once in awhile about what it will be like when you "join the majority." That's another way of saying, consider "the alternative." A hymn that is part of Night Prayer in the Liturgy of the Hours (the Divine Office or Breviary, as it is sometimes called) says it nicely, "We praise you, Father, for your gifts/Of dusk and nightfall over earth,/Foreshadowing the mystery/of death that leads to endless day."

You are going to experience "endless day" once you "join the majority." You are going to be eternally awake and eternally aware. The English word *enthusiasm* comes from two Greek words *en theos* meaning "in God." That will be your experience. So you might start thinking now of what eternal enthusiasm will be like for you. And think of the generations that have gone on before. You will meet them all. You will know the saints to whom you prayed, the historical figures you admired, and millions of others whom you never knew existed, and you will be reunited with those you loved the most when they shared space and life with you on this Earth. They will all be part of your eternal awareness. As will the mysteries of faith and the "mysteries" of things like calculus and chemistry that you never managed to translate from textbook print to mental assimilation.

So go ahead now and let yourself say, "I can hardly wait!"

13.

The Art of Listening

In our present-day cell phone era, we seem to be always and everywhere "all ears" all the time. Cell phones are banned from classrooms and silenced in theaters, clubs, and restaurants. But across all divisions of age, class, and sex, mobile phones have given the human ear a degree of anatomical prominence it has never known before.

Nonetheless, just because it is, there is no reason to conclude that the ear will always be used. "Let anyone with ears to hear listen!" (Mark 4:9) is a biblical prompting that bears repeating in our day. There seems to be a lot more talking and a lot less listening these days, even though we all want to be "in the know."

Many years ago a little boy told me that he had figured out why you have grandparents when you're growing up: "So that you'll have someone who will listen to you," he said. Not all that flattering to his parents, but not all that wide of the mark either. He's a successful lawyer now; recently he called my attention to the following item in the business press.

James J. Schiro, CEO of Zurich Financial Services, was asked by the *New York Times* (May 10, 2009), "What is the most important leadership lesson you've learned?" His reply: "It's the ability to listen, and to make people understand that you are listening to them. Make them feel that they are making a contribution, and then you make a decision. You've got to have a sense of inclusiveness." This is from the "Corner

Office" feature that appears in the Sunday business section of the *Times*. Note that listening is, in this CEO's view, the most important leadership lesson he learned along his way to the top. That's a remarkable statement.

If you are in a position of responsibility and you open yourself to listening, you will, on occasion, "get an earful." But you can always filter out the vengeful and unfair portions of what unfriendly critics might pour into your auditory canal. To shut yourself off from hearing the rest of what they might have to say is not wise, however, especially if you are a leader. For some leaders, selective listening is a form of self-defense. The flow of information is constant; they just can't process it all. Tuning out every now and then is a noise-abatement device that keeps them sane. But if we experience a widespread decline in what I'll call personal acoustics—a loss of interest in hearing what others have to say—we will inevitably experience a decline in effective leadership. This is happening these days in many areas of organizational life.

I'm most concerned about it happening in the Church. There are fewer religious leaders than there are business and political leaders in the United States, of course. But if religious leaders decide to improve the acoustics in their respective spheres of responsibility, not only will a noticeable improvement in church leadership follow, but also the Church might find itself setting good leadership example for the state and other areas of organizational life. Political leaders tend to listen to citizens and donors because they need votes and campaign contributions. Business leaders tend to listen to shareholders and customers because they need investors and customers. Church leaders don't need votes, but they do need contributions to support their ministries. They also need to listen so that their message and ministries will be on the mark, meeting people's needs. Like leaders anywhere, if church leaders choose not to listen, they are choosing not to lead.

14.

What Are We Doing About the Priest Shortage?

Sociologists have surveyed college-age Catholics regarding their attitudes toward careers in church ministry. They find an enormous reservoir of generosity and genuine interest in ministry, but not ordained ministry. When researchers probe the reasons why, they identify several institutional barriers: (1) celibacy (the sexual revolution is still having a negative impact on vocations to priesthood), (2) the requirement that priests make a permanent lifelong commitment (if there were something like the military model with a 20-year enlistment, some say that priesthood would be more attractive to them), and (3) the exclusion of women from holy orders (which even men take as a proxy for institutional injustice in the Church). Researchers also identify a tendency on the part of the young to remain uncommitted, a cultural hesitation to make permanent commitments. Parents today are not storming heaven with prayers that their offspring will be called to priesthood or religious life. Without parental encouragement, the young are far less likely to consider priesthood and religious life.

Among the personal effects left behind by Father John W. Tynan, SJ, after his death in 1960, was a letter from his father, received shortly after young Jack Tynan left his home in Jersey City, NJ, to enter the Jesuit novitiate in 1919. His dad wrote:

> You gave me one of the greatest joys of my life when you told me you had joined the Jesuits. I never mentioned a

vocation to you because I believe the Almighty reserves calling men to the priesthood to Himself. Years before the Holy Hour was begun in St. Bridget's, I used to have one on my own on Saturday nights. I never could meditate, so I prayed and hoped and begged and cried, yes, and sometimes I fell asleep, all in one hour. You were often the subject of my thoughts. I said many a time to our blessed Lord, "I'll waive the pleasure of ever seeing his back at the altar as a priest, only call him—for Kalamazoo, or Hong Kong, or Jersey City."

Shortly after writing that letter, Mr. Tynan died. And with him went an era characterized not only by the Holy Hour and the back at the altar, but also by tears and prayers focused on the call to priesthood for one's son.

Why don't fathers pray today as Jack Tynan's father did? Where is the Church that fostered such prayer? The Church is still present in our midst, but its sociological surroundings are markedly different. They are splitting at several prominent seams: (1) Many men have left the priesthood (thus raising the question "Why?"); (2) the tragic evidence of scandal and misconduct in the priesthood (prompting the "steer-clear-of-that-crowd" reaction); (3) the debate about the desirability of having a married Catholic clergy (suggesting the question "Why not?"); and (4) talk about the possibility of women priests (keeping alive the question of whether this is something that would be impossible for an all-powerful God to bring about).

We need more priests to serve God's people by proclaiming God's Word; ministering the sacraments; and, along with lay associates, staffing the social, educational, and health services the Church provides. We need more female ministers too—lay and religious.

Leadership in the Church has to take a good look at those barriers—the institutional barriers to entry—that are discouraging the generous young from considering priesthood. And all of us have to pray for a solution to the priest shortage as we offer prayers of thanks for the unsung women who are keeping the boat afloat right now.

Because there has never been a Roman Catholic priest who was not also the son of a woman, it would be wise for the Church to be both attentive to and appreciative of female members, while taking care not to anger or alienate them so that they might be more inclined to encourage their sons to consider a vocation to the priesthood.

15.

Effective Parish Leadership

There's a lot of talk about leadership these days, especially during political campaigns that seem never to end. But leadership talk appears to be happening more frequently in business as well as government, and in church as well as state. I found it encouraging to see an emphasis on leadership in a Saturday morning meeting a few years ago at Corpus Christi Catholic parish in suburban Philadelphia where many from surrounding parishes gathered to discuss leadership, involvement, community, and spirituality in parish life. I was invited to offer some keynote thoughts.

There is a distinction, I pointed out, between leadership and management, and that distinction was not news to this predominantly lay assembly. They agreed that management deals with complexity and leadership deals with change.

Although it is sometimes said that you lead people and manage things, I reminded them that the late Peter Drucker, an expert on business management, wrote that, "Management deals with people, their values, their growth and develop-

ment—and this makes it [the study of management] a human-
ity" (*The New Realities*, Harper & Row, 1989).

Aware, however, that leadership deals with change, the
parish leaders in this assembly realized that any attempt to
bring about change will draw resistance; they know that
most humans prefer to live in the immediate past. So those
who want to lead, I suggested, have to be persuasive com-
municators. It is more important, of course, for a leader to
have integrity and creativity, but if you don't write and speak
well, you are probably not going to lead effectively in a
parish or anywhere else.

Although the emphasis at the Corpus Christi gathering
was on parish leadership, it was natural to think of political
and business leaders, even military leaders, as we considered that there's something to be said for "followership,"
too, but it was up to the subgroups in this gathering to
decide how best to generate more involvement and wider
participation on the part of parishioners in parish activities.

I mentioned that I had just read an interesting book
titled *Counselor: A Life at the Edge of History* (HarperCollins,
2008), by Ted Sorensen, special counsel to President John F.
Kennedy and best known, perhaps, as Kennedy's chief speech
writer. Speaking of Kennedy as leader, Sorenson writes:

> JFK was a wonderful boss. We never argued, quar-
> reled, shouted, or swore at each other. He never
> bawled me out. He never asked me to lie to anyone.
> He never misled or lied to me....When mistakes
> occurred, whether in his campaign or in his presi-
> dency, he never blamed me or anyone else on his
> staff, or disavowed me or others when under political
> or journalistic pressure. To the contrary, he always
> protected and defended us. When a speech of his on
> which I had worked went well, or a political task I

had undertaken for him succeeded, he often tele-
phoned me the next day with profuse thanks.

During any political season, people assess leadership
qualities. Most of us like a friendly leader. We want evidence
that the would-be leader's ears are not purely ornamental;
we want to be heard by the one we're being asked to follow.
We want honesty, integrity, and veracity as well as energy in
our leaders.

Servant Leadership (Paulist Press, 25th anniversary edition, 2002), by Robert K. Greenleaf, is a book I often recom-
mend. That title is a particularly apt description for any form
of leadership in a parish. Years ago in a panel discussion at the
University of Notre Dame, Professor Dennis Goulet listed the
following three essentials of Christian leadership: availability,
accountability, and vulnerability. He was right on target.

Where parish leadership displays those three qualities,
can engaged followership be far behind?

16.

Real Presence Is a Four-Sided Reality

I've given a lot of thought to published reports of fewer
Catholics showing up for Mass on Sundays; some of them
checking out of the Church altogether. I wonder whether or
not they miss the Eucharist. And that raises the question of
the effectiveness of Catholic catechesis relative to the centrality of Eucharist to Catholic life.

As those thoughts were running through my mind in
2011, I came across two publications. One is a bimonthly
magazine of the St. Petersburg, FL, diocese called *Gathered,
Nourished, Sent*. The January–February 2009 issue has an
article by the local bishop Robert N. Lynch titled "The

Living Eucharist: How Much Do We Really Believe It, and What Does It All Mean?"

Good questions.

What does the "real presence" of Christ in the Eucharist really mean? And if it means anything at all, why are growing numbers of Catholics saying, in effect, "No thanks; not interested"?

The other publication is the January 2011 issue of *Worship*, which carried a long review article by the editor, Kevin Seasoltz, OSB, of a book by his Benedictine confrere and noted liturgist Ansgar Chupungco titled *What, Then, Is Liturgy? Musings and Memoir* (Liturgical Press, 2010).

Bishop Lynch points out that "God is present to us in three ways: (1) in his word, (2) in his body and blood in the Eucharist, and (3) in one another." Father Chupungco sees the Lord Jesus as being present in four ways, not only in the Eucharistic elements (really present under the appearance of bread and wine) "but also in the presence of the priest through whose ministry he [Christ] now offers what he [Christ] formerly offered on the cross." The third way in which Christ is present is when the Word of God is proclaimed in the assembly—the readings from Scripture. And the fourth is Christ's presence "in the assembly of the faithful who are truly the Body of Christ." Wherever two or three are gathered in my name, I'm right there in their midst, said Jesus.

These four modes of Christ's presence in the eucharistic liturgy are, to say the least, insufficiently understood and vastly underappreciated in Catholic worshipping assemblies today. This four-way real presence should be a four-way stop sign halting the exodus researchers are tracking and journalists are reporting in the Catholic Church.

For the good of the Church, catechetical repair work is needed. Pastoral attention must be paid to this problem. Priests and bishops can "proclaim," but they and other teachers must "explain" the four-way presence of Christ in the Eucharist.

It takes faith, of course, to see Christ where only bread and wine are visible, but that's what faith does for the believer. It gives sight where vision fails.

It will take a lot of faith for the people to see Jesus in the person of an unsmiling priest or bishop, even those who try to make themselves more presentable at the altar and less unworthy of their calling to serve the faithful by offering sacrifice.

That sacrifice is also a meal and the people have to attend to their role in gathering around the table not as isolated worshippers, but as brothers and sisters in the Lord who recognize Christ in one another as well as in the breaking of the bread.

Better readers (trained and auditioned) and improved sound systems can enhance awareness that Christ is present in the word (i.e., in the liturgical event of proclaiming the word) as will repetition of words and phrases from the Scripture just proclaimed in the follow-up homily, which should be an extension of the proclamation.

All will agree that much work needs to be done. Each of us can say, let it begin with me.

17.

War and the Christian Conscience

Long before peace studies made any significant headway into the Catholic college curriculum, Professor Joseph Fahey had an impressive program going at Manhattan College. He's been at it for over forty years. Instead of having just one year's experience forty times, his teaching and research over the years produced annual growth in his understanding and appreciation of the relationship between the Christian conscience and the question of war. He emerges from the experience with something quite important to say.

With the release of his book *War & the Christian Conscience: Where Do You Stand?* (Orbis Books, 2005), Professor Fahey's masterful pedagogy is available to a larger audience. Widespread confusion and unease at home over America's involvement in the wars in Iraq and Afghanistan make this book more than timely; it is necessary.

Fahey's approach is direct: "This is a book intended for the general reader who may never have personally decided where he or she stands on war." Through many years of teaching and lecturing on issues of war and peace, he says,

> I have found that many people mistake their culture for their conscience. They think they should follow the views of their nation, or their religion, or their family. I have found that very few people have ever seriously examined the issue of war and come to their own personal decision with regard to it.

For those willing to engage their minds in an unemotional examination of the moral issues associated with war, this book provides the searchlight, compass, and road map. It is intended to be a help for the inquiring, independent mind, not an instruction for the passive, unreflective person. Moreover, because "Christianity does not speak with one voice on the morality of war," it is obvious that the Christian conscience is likely to need some help in addressing the challenge raised by the subtitle of this book: *Where Do You Stand?*

The author begins by getting an imaginary classroom full of students immediately engaged with a hypothetical presidential announcement that, in order to meet our national commitment "to spread freedom and democracy to such nations as Iran, Venezuela, Burundi, Cuba, Uzbekistan, North Korea, Columbia, and Syria," the military draft will be restored for men and women—no exemptions—and "all college students will report for basic training at the end of the semester after their nineteenth birthday." Readers willing to take a seat in that classroom will become similarly engaged with the question of conscientious objection or participation in military service.

Through chapters dealing with the formation of conscience, the history of pacifism, the traditional "just war" doctrine, the notion of "total war" as evidenced in the Crusades ("God's Wars"), the existence of military religious orders, the Inquisitions ("Crusades at Home"), the Conquistadors ("Crusades Abroad"), the Fascist security state, and the contemporary threat of terrorism, the reader gains an appreciation of the complexity of the war question.

Fahey examines the desirability and possibility of establishing some transnational body capable of fostering peace in the world community by providing a forum for dispute resolution. In *Pacem in Terris* (1963), Pope John XXIII issued a call for a "world-wide public authority" that could do just that. Today, that goal seems to me to be not so wild a dream as those who have unworthy motives for postponing it pretend.

In any case, Joe Fahey continues to serve the cause of peace by reciting history and raising the right questions about war.

PART TWO

Business and Politics

18.

From Bubble Gum to Business Ethics

I participate in a monthly roundtable discussion on workplace spirituality and business ethics with about a dozen midcareer executives, who are all alumni of Catholic colleges. They want to support one another in relating religious faith to business responsibilities. A recent topic for discussion was veracity.

Just as integrity means living truthfully, veracity means speaking truthfully. Veracity, these executives understood, is truthfulness. They were all aware of that, but they wanted to reflect together on how they learned honesty and truthfulness and how they might now foster a commitment in their offspring to these values. One of the participants recalled a lesson learned from his father and shared it with the group.

"I was only eight or nine," he said, "and I was sitting outside a neighborhood candy store when a Fleers bubble-gum truck pulled up to deliver a shipment. When the driver climbed back into the cab and drove off, a large box of bubble gum fell off the back of the truck. I ran out and picked it up. The truck was gone; the gum was mine.

"I carried the container home and shared the news of my find with my mother. She told me not to open the box and that I should show it to my father when he came home from work. I did exactly that, and my father asked, 'When are you going to return it?' 'Return it?' I exclaimed. 'It's mine; I found it.'

"'No it's not,' said his father. 'Put that box in your wagon and take it back to the Fleers plant.'"

He told the youngster how to get there; it was about a mile and a half away. A few days later a letter arrived from the president of Fleers thanking the boy for his good deed.

About eight years later this same boy, now a high school student, wanted to find a summer job. His father suggested that he apply at Fleers. He did. They remembered him. He worked there for two successive summers before moving on to college.

Instead of becoming a bubble-gum bandit, this young man became an early beneficiary of a lesson in business ethics. He carried it with him, he said, into his career as a CPA and chief financial officer in several corporations. In one of his jobs, he noticed that his employer—a manufacturer of construction trailers—had accumulated about a quarter of a million dollars in unclaimed deposits. Those who rented the trailers failed to ask for their deposit back once the trailer had been returned. He didn't get a standing ovation when he pointed out to the executive group that they were not just holding, but spending, other people's money. But they agreed to return all deposits, even when not asked, and thus not only preserved their corporate integrity, but also avoided possible criminal prosecution.

Others in the group learned similar lessons at the dinner table or in automobile rides with their fathers. They learned that there may be unpleasant consequences if you tell the truth, but, as the saying goes, "the truth will always out." They also learned that the truth teller will always have a place to stand, a soul to claim, and a peace of mind that can never be taken away.

And, before dispersing, as they considered topics for future discussion, one member of this group expressed regret that families gather together far less frequently for dinner these days; as a consequence, he noted, fewer lessons in business ethics are being taught at home.

19.

Dealing with Job-Search Discouragement

Several years ago, within weeks of each other, Microsoft eliminated five thousand jobs and IBM notified an undisclosed number of employees that they would be subject to a "resource action." That's a new term for layoffs. It had been happening in virtually all sectors of the economy. Hundreds of thousands were out of work and looking.

Some job seekers find themselves for the first time asking someone else for help. They find this distasteful. Unaccustomed as they are to asking for help, they are even less prepared for the refusal and rejection those requests will draw. Not flat-out rejections; those will be rare. But letters have a way of being set aside, resumes get lost, promised calls become promises broken; and the "anything-I-can-do-to-help" messages become forced or muted, not followed up by prompt delivery. This leaves the job seeker even more alone and much discouraged.

Beneath these surface-level disappointments lies a substratum of discouragement in many that calls out for the durability of hope, a call that does not ordinarily get an immediate response. Hope is needed to provide the courage to endure.

Those who experience job loss need immediate and repeated assurance that they have not been laid off from life, despite the negative psychological signals they are receiving.

Back in the 1960s when college students were supposed to be unreflective activists, Jim Beek, a student at Loyola College in Baltimore, wrote a poem called "The Catharsis" for the winter 1968 issue of *Ignis*, the campus literary quarterly, that speaks to the heart of the problem the person searching for work has to confront. The poem opened with the line, "I awoke in the silent fist of the night gagging on loneliness." Then, several lines later, Beek writes: "And the fear that my existence wasn't doing/anyone any good/Was under my fifth rib." So he prays "to a god who would have nothing to do with a stained glass window," and gets this reply: "Son—/This is the pain that lets you know you're alive."

The fear that your existence isn't "doing anyone any good" adds a lot of heavy freight to a job seeker's discouragement. If, as the psychologists remind us, depression is inverted anger (i.e., anger turned in on itself) discouragement might be thought of as an aching awareness of not being needed. The pain is there, "under my fifth rib," alright, but it can serve as a reminder that the job seeker is alive, a full member of the human race, ready to contribute, and walking a path of persistence that leads to another job.

There's the word—*persistence*. Discouragement erodes it, undercuts it, tries to smother it. Discouragement puts the fire out. The really discouraged person stops looking. The persistent person never gives up.

Persistence can activate the optimism that lies hidden in the inner person, somewhere in the nervous system, ready to spring. But you have to try it to become convinced. You have to believe that the other side of every "out" is "in," and that any exit is an entrance in reverse. Every ouster is the starting gate for a comeback.

You deal with discouragement by not giving up. You simply decide not to live your life "back there;" dredging up the past can be a real depressant. You decide to take life one day at a time. You ask yourself: What is most important in my life right now? And you know, as you look at your potential, your family responsibilities, and the economic realities of your existence, that the most important thing for you right now is getting a job. Add your personal Amen to William Faulkner's line in his Nobel Prize acceptance speech: "I believe that man ["woman" would, of course, be specifically included today] will not merely endure: he will prevail."

20.

Job Creation Is a Civic Responsibility

There is no better social welfare program that I can think of than a full-employment economy. Really full—everyone who is able and looking for work, everyone who wants a job can find one. When that's the case, marriages and family life are stronger, crime is lower, homelessness is down, substance abuse is less of a problem, and schools, especially secondary schools, are better and busier because they are engaged with students who are motivated by the realization that employment goals are within their reach.

Jobs are key. It is not encouraging, then, to hear talk about a jobless recovery from the economic meltdown that started in 2008 and became known as the Great Recession. Without more jobs, recovery is an illusion; indicators of societal health will remain less than robust. School dropouts will have no employment net to catch them; they will hit the street. Social malaise will spread.

But how can a nation that has watched its manufacturing and agricultural employment numbers fall for more than fifty years hope now to provide meaningful work to high school dropouts? How can the service sector provide work for relatively unskilled and not well-educated job seekers? How can older Americans, concerned with higher health-care costs and diminished pension income, find employment security during their lengthening stretch of senior years? No easy answers to these and related questions.

President Barack Obama, of course, was looking for answers as pundits reminded him that failure to produce more jobs would cost him reelection in 2012. No one can fairly put full blame on him for economic conditions, but anyone can choose to punish him if economic conditions do not improve. That's part of the risk that goes with the presidential territory.

The president spoke often to this issue, urging banks to lend to small businesses, discussing tax incentives to employers who are willing to expand payrolls, and providing funding for public works projects to replace and repair decaying bridge and highway infrastructure while attending to water and sewer needs in both urban and rural areas.

"To move is to produce" is an economic truism. So, more movement of people and products in the air, on the roads and rails, and over the water will surely strengthen the gross domestic product. But who has the responsibility for getting our great economic engine moving again? All of us do.

I like what I saw in a news report a couple of years ago that the University of Delaware purchased an idle Chrysler plant in Newark, DE, and began refitting it to become a practical, impact-focused research center with an eye on job creation. University president Patrick T. Harker prepped for his job by serving for a decade as dean of the entrepreneurial Wharton School of Business at the University of Pennsylvania. The state of Delaware has a university that is worth watching now as it attempts to show the nation how to apply impact research to the great challenge of job creation.

I was equally impressed when I read that billionaire entrepreneur Warren Buffett did himself and the nation a favor by buying the Burlington Northern Santa Fe Corp., the nation's largest railroad operator. Buffett paid $26.3 billion, putting his money to work in a company that "can't move its jobs off-shore."

Innovation and entrepreneurship are needed to make sure that ours will not be a jobless recovery from the Great Recession. Creative thinking and prudent risk taking are civic responsibilities in a nation that needs jobs.

21.

Crisis in the Economy

Few people think of it this way, but we live in a faith-based economy. Not religious faith, to be sure, but faith nonetheless.

Religious language without religious meaning has dominated the headlines since 2008: "Confidence in Financial Markets Plummets," we read. Notice that "con" is English for *cum,* the Latin preposition meaning "with," and *fides* is Latin for "faith." So confidence means "with faith." Whenever confidence in markets takes a hike, faith has slipped away before it.

The "credit" markets were frozen, business analysts warned. Well, "credit" derives from the Latin *credo,* "I believe;" and there again, when credit stops flowing, faith has preceded lending into the deep freeze. Banks stop lending to other banks, and to business or individual borrowers, because confidence in their ability to repay has vanished.

Interesting, isn't it, to recall that when a company was formed in Boston some years ago to manage other people's financial assets, the founders decided to call it "Fidelity." You'll find "trust," "providence," and other terms from the vocabulary of religious faith sprinkled throughout business directories listing banks (depository or investment banks), insurance, and mortgage companies. Religious faith would have you entrust yourself to God; secular faith involves mutual trust between buyer and seller, lender and borrower in the marketplace.

There are many markets in the world of finance. Best known, perhaps, is the stock market, but that's not where the problem was in the Great Recession of 2008. To the extent that speculation displaces investment, and greed drives decisions to buy or sell, there will be speculative "bubbles" in the stock market and cause for genuine concern. Indeed, stock market fluctuations signal stress in the nation's economic nervous system. But our problems in the Great Recession related chiefly to the credit markets and had their underlying causes in overpriced real estate and the subprime mortgage loans foisted upon willing but unqualified borrowers by greedy and profit-seeking lenders.

As the whole world knows, all this led to a legislative crisis and executive leadership challenge in our national government. Neither then Treasury Secretary Paulson, nor President Bush was familiar, I suspect, with a classic principle of Catholic social teaching known as the Principle of Subsidiarity. This principle is designed to keep government in its place. In essence, it says that no decision should be taken at a higher level of organization that can be taken as efficiently and effectively at a lower level. This principle was articulated by Pope Pius XI in 1931 in *Quadragesimo Anno* ("On Reconstructing the Social Order") marking the fortieth anniversary of Pope Leo XIII's *Rerum Novarum*.

Although they may never have heard of it, both Secretary Paulson and President Bush did, however, use the language of subsidiarity when they argued that the federal government had to come to the "rescue" because the problem was "too big" to be handled efficiently and effectively at any other level in our economic system. Only government, what some critics scornfully call Big Government, was up to the job. The president and treasury secretary were right. The Senate immediately agreed and the House of Representatives eventually came around to seeing the light.

This is not Socialism any more than a New Deal initiative in the 1930s, creating the Home Owners Loan Corporation during the Great Depression, was Socialism. Much repair work remains to be done in our national economy. The tradition of Catholic social thought can help. Those responsible for fixing our problems must have competence (knowledge of economics and finance) and conscience (ethical principles). Faith in themselves will help. Faith in God is not to be overlooked.

Ideology at either extreme of the political spectrum will only get in the way.

22.

The Future of Social Security

They don't call it the "third rail of American politics" for nothing!

How many times have you heard older voters say, "Don't fiddle around with my Social Security"? "Privatize the system," say some younger and less risk-adverse workers. They are troubled with the twin concerns of anticipated low returns (relative to stock market performance) on their Social Security payments, and the shrinking ratio of working contributors to retired beneficiaries.

The George W. Bush White House favored privatization of Social Security, even though on their watch 401(k) accounts, the popular private retirement savings plan, started losing money for the first time in their then 20-year history. Many who had taken the 401(k) option had made unwise investment decisions.

Social Security still needs attention and every time the issue arises in political debate, sparks, fur, and fists begin to fly. "Pay-as-you-go" entitlements describe the social security system in most advanced nations. But what happens when the ratio of workers to retirees (fewer workers supporting more retirees) signals an unmanageable payment burden on the workers? That day is not all that far away in America (its arrival date depends on the assumptions of those who are making the calculations). Hence, the need now for serious thinking about the health of the so-called Social Security trust fund and the future of the whole Social Security system, not just retirement, but disability, survivors, and health-care benefits as well.

This debate is primarily about insurance—social insurance, where the risk must be socialized, that is, spread widely enough among the strong to protect the weakest members of society. It is not about private investment, so comparisons with the stock market are largely irrelevant. To the extent that the young, strong, and affluent take a privatizing exit, the system is weakened, and the weak are made more vulnerable.

Anyone interested in this debate should go back and take a look at a book by former commerce secretary and retired investment banker Peter Peterson, *Gray Dawn: How the Coming Age Wave Will Transform America—and the World* (Times Books, 1999). It offers six basic strategies for the consideration of policy makers. All six deserve attention today.

- Lower retirement ages and longer life spans add to the weight of benefit costs. So reduce dependency among the elderly by encouraging longer work lives. (Worker strikes in France when this policy change was under serious consideration in 2010 serve to remind how this proposal will meet resistance.)
- In order to attend to the problem of the shrinking denominator (fewer active workers), encourage more work from the nonelderly, either by getting working-age citizens to work more or by increas-

ing the inflow of working-age immigrants. (How will that go over in Arizona?)

- Raise more numerous and productive children in order to spread the cost burden over a larger and more affluent rising generation. The affluence, presumably, will be a function of productivity, which, in turn, depends on better education.
- Stress filial obligation, and hope that tomorrow's grown children will be more willing to support, through familial and informal devices, their own elderly parents.
- Target benefits on the basis of financial need, and this will increase the "carrying capacity" of the younger generation by reducing benefits to the affluent elderly, who would be "means tested" in order to qualify.
- Require people to provide in advance for their own old-age dependency by saving and investing more of their income during their work lives.

Nobody said it is going to be easy! We have to face up to hard choices, and we have to remember that insurance and investment are horses of altogether different hues.

23.

Responding to the Crisis in Haiti

There are big differences between leaders and managers. Managers administer; they mind the store. But leaders innovate. Managers hold the fort, leaders develop new frontiers. The manager imitates; the leader originates.

Ed Rendell, then governor of Pennsylvania, proved himself to be an innovative leader in his response to the earthquake crisis in Haiti in 2010. A consummate politician always in touch with the people, Rendell responded immediately to a plea from two Pennsylvania sisters who ran an orphanage in earthquake-shattered Haiti. As a result, fifty-four orphans were airlifted to Pittsburgh to await adoption and, because of the attention this got in the news media, renewed interest was stimulated in adopting American children languishing in Pennsylvania orphanages.

The two Pennsylvanians working in the Haiti orphanage, Jamie and Ali McMurtrie, made Blackberry contact with Rendell and others when the disaster struck. The earthquake occurred on a Tuesday. The governor was on the ground in Haiti for six hours the following Monday, having gotten a charter plane from Republic Airways and assembling a rescue team from the University of Pittsburgh Medical Center, the Red Cross, and Catholic Charities of Pittsburgh.

U.S. Congressman Jason Altmire, a Democrat from western Pennsylvania was on the flight; he helped with White House and State Department contacts to obtain visas for the children.

A neonatologist who was part of the medical team on the rescue flight, told the *Pittsburgh Post Gazette,* "I felt a little safer with Governor Rendell on board, and I don't think any of what transpired would have, if the governor had not been on board. Clearance for the plane to land, getting the kids released with special visas; I think without him, none of it happens" (*Pittsburgh Post Gazette*, January 20, 2010).

Rendell agreed to accompany the Pittsburgh group after Haiti's ambassador to the United States told him that his help might be needed to cut through any red tape on the orphans' behalf. The ambassador said, "If problems crop up, you are the only one to get it done," said Rendell at a press conference upon his return. "To some extent, that proved true." The objective was to get two-and-a-half tons of medical supplies, which were donated by the University of Pittsburgh Medical Center, down to Haiti, and to bring the children back. The governor and his team accomplished both.

As the rest of us contributed whatever we could to the relief effort, we were forced to start thinking longer term about eliminating poverty in Haiti. As David Brooks pointed out in the *New York Times*, when a magnitude 7.0 earthquake hit the San Francisco Bay area on October 17, 1989 (remember seeing it as you watched the World Series game between the Oakland Athletics and San Francisco Giants?), sixty-three people were killed. When an earthquake of the exact same magnitude struck near Port-au-Prince, Haiti, on January 12, 2010, uncounted thousands died. The difference? Poverty.

Flimsy construction, a weak economy, the colonial legacy, illiteracy, and widespread political corruption describe the collapsed infrastructure of a broken nation. Rebuilding it will require strategically applied economic assistance, education, engineering, political stability, and integrity in government. It will also take a lot of time.

Locate the Caribbean island of Hispaniola on your map and notice that it contains two sovereign nations: Haiti and the Dominican Republic. Investigate the disparities—economic, political, cultural—between them, and then give some thought to what is both possible and achievable in the monumental task of Haitian reconstruction.

Management won't do it. Leadership might. But leadership without intellectual resources and a global commitment to social justice will come up short. There's also need for a higher power.

Recall the televised images of devastation in Haiti and heed this suggestion: "The world is fragile, handle with prayer."

24.

Health-Care Finance Reform

President Barack Obama invited an impressive group of legislators, lobbyists, policy experts, and those who provide and consume health-care services to the White House in March 2010. He urged them to put their heads together to come up with solutions to the nation's health-care problem. As the debate began, I thought all should be aware that defining the problem correctly is an essential first step. If policy proposals fail to focus on health-care *finance* reform, they will miss the mark. And, sad to say, they did.

If this issue, one that will surely define the Obama presidency, is ever going to be resolved, the word *finance* must modify the word *reform* in this great debate that will continue for many years. The two main problems relate to cost and coverage. As a percentage of gross domestic product, health-care is costing us far too much. And the range of health-care insurance coverage in this nation, in the absence of reform, is far too narrow. Cost and coverage, are the issues, along with the maintenance of quality. That's the challenge: How to bring costs down while retaining quality, and how to make insurance coverage extend to everyone. Health-care finance reform is the route to a solution.

During his years in the White House, President Clinton tried and failed to address this issue. He put the project in the hands of then First Lady Hillary Rodham Clinton and Ira Magaziner, a White House domestic policy adviser. They worked behind closed doors, invited no legislators to their planning sessions, lost the public relations battle to the health-care insurance industry's TV ads (remember Harry and Louise?), and produced an administration bill that was dead on arrival when it reached the Congress.

Mr. Obama opened his 2010 White House meeting to representatives of all interested parties and to all points of view. He clearly learned an important lesson from the Clinton experience. Nor was he unaware that as far back as Harry Truman attempts have been made without success to extend health-care insurance to all Americans. He was exercising good leadership in raising the issue, fully aware that there is no easy or inexpensive solution.

By virtue of his economic recovery bill, promptly enacted into law, Mr. Obama designated $20 billion to begin modernizing (i.e., converting to electronic form) medical records. Electronic record keeping will surely reduce costs and help avoid medical errors. Moreover, the president's budget set aside $634 billion for a start in providing coverage over ten years to some of the uninsured. What is called universal coverage would presumably mean a single-payer system. This would be government-paid, Medicare-like basic coverage for all Americans, allowing those who want, and can afford it, to purchase additional coverage in the private market.

The president did not advocate a single-payer system. He wanted private insurers to remain in the game. But he also wanted rates charged by private insurers to be affordable and he wanted to keep the existing fee-for-service system of provision to hold those fees down.

Providers often complain about Medicare reimbursement rates, but few Medicare recipients complain about their coverage. In my view, there is a directional signal there or a tea leaf still waiting to be read. It points to a future where there will be universal coverage and a regulated fee-for-service system (with a set range of fees approved by professional peers) along with cost monitoring (again by peers) of charges made by hospitals and clinics. This addresses both cost and coverage, and it protects quality. In a nutshell, this describes health-care finance reform—a political hot potato and an as-yet unmet social justice challenge.

25.

Campaign Finance Reform

Crucial words can slip in and out of political debate in a most curious way. Take *finance,* for example.

As I pointed out in the previous essay, when former First Lady Hillary Rodham Clinton and White House domestic policy adviser Ira Magaziner began working, furtively some would say, on Health-Care Finance Reform at the beginning of the first Clinton term, the word *finance* soon dropped out of the discussion. All we heard about was "health-care reform."

Opponents of the then brand-new Clinton administration, interested in delaying or defeating any fresh White House initiatives, openly ridiculed the suggestion that the best health-care system in the world was in need of reform. Even without the "Harry and Louise" TV commercials, millions of Americans became uneasy and afraid that reformers were going to mess up a system that had been working quite well for them. Lost from view were the 44-or-more-million citizens who had no health insurance (a finance issue), and that dollar outlays for health care, as a portion of our gross domestic product, were hitting 14 percent and growing (another finance concern).

As one who thought health-care finance reform was (and still is) necessary, I was astonished in the midst of this policy debate to hear Mrs. Clinton tell the Economic Club of Washington in a luncheon address, that she realized that the reform proposals would bring "Socialism" into our system, but that the time had come. "Socialism" to an Economic Club audience?

We all know what happened to Health-Care Finance Reform in the Clinton administration.

Later we started talking about Campaign Finance Reform. Despite occasional journalistic shortcuts taken by columnists and headline writers, the word *finance* stayed alive in this debate. Curiously, the fact that finance remains a prominent part of the picture helps to explain why the House of Representatives (which voted for reform in the past when members knew the Senate would kill it) found itself in a quandary about what to do when the reform ball bounced into its court after Senate passage of the McCain–Feingold bill, a tough campaign finance reform measure. This now sounds like ancient history.

The word *finance* remains as a troubling reminder that many a political ox, running with packs of Democratic donkeys and Republican elephants, will surely be gored in the future. And when your ox is at risk of being hit, you begin to see things differently.

There are indeed some First Amendment considerations to be taken into account in the matter of limiting financial contributions to political campaigns. "Money talks," as we all know, and there are some honest concerns about suppressing speech when clamps are put on political contributions. But the words of Carl Sandburg ("What Shall He Tell That Son?"), originating in an altogether different context, are applicable today to campaigns in our representative democracy: "Tell him too much money has killed men/And left them dead years before burial."

Political campaigns at every level are awash in money. Most of our politicians are honest and our democratic system is, I think, the best in the world. So-called soft money, unregulated contributions given to political parties (for redirection in support of specific campaigns), can seriously damage the integrity of both the players and the playing fields.

Don't be surprised if courage eventually prevails and serious campaign finance reform is enacted into law. But that expectation might be another instance of hope triumphing over reality. In any given session of Congress that one crucial word that just won't go away—finance—can explain inaction. Why? Because you're talking about money. Money itself talks, as we all know. And when it talks about campaign finance reform, it has a way of saying, loud and clear, No way!

26.

Countercultural Catholic Education for Business

Three days of spirited discussion in mid-July 2010 between and among Jesuit business school educators focused on the challenge of preparing students for business leadership in a culture of consumerism, materialism, and me-first individualism.

Approximately one hundred "Colleagues in Jesuit Business Education," met at Marquette University to assess the consistency between what they are doing and the Ignatian principles that underlie their schools. Ignatius of Loyola wrote in his book of *Spiritual Exercises* that the three steps to genuine success are poverty as opposed to riches; insults or contempt as opposed to the honor of this world; humility as opposed to pride.

"Consider," says Ignatius, "how the Lord of all the world chooses so many persons, apostles, disciples, and the like. He sends them throughout the whole world, to spread his doctrine among people of every state and condition.

"Consider the address which Christ our Lord makes to all his servants and friends whom he is sending on this expedition. He recommends that they endeavor to aid all persons, by attracting them, first, to the most perfect spiritual poverty and also, if the Divine Majesty should be served and should wish to choose them for it, even to no less a degree of actual poverty; and second, by attracting them to a desire for reproaches and contempt, since from these results humility.

"In this way there will be three steps: the first, poverty in opposition to riches; the second, reproaches or contempt in opposition to honor from the world; and the third, humility in opposition to pride. Then from these three steps they should induce people to all the other virtues."

To the eye of faith, acceptance of the genuine Ignatian vision and values—a refusal to be possessed by one's possessions—will be seen as a form of liberation that frees a person to become an effective leader. To the secular eye, this makes no sense. How, then, can it make sense in a modern business school?

A back-office service company SEI Investments in Oak, PA, holds up the word *humbition* for praise and imitation. "At SEI, the most effective leaders exude a blend of humility and ambition—humbition—that relies on the power of persuasion rather than formal authority" (see William C. Taylor and Polly LaBarre, *Mavericks at Work*, Harper, 2008).

Humility, as demonstrated in the life of Christ, is a highly desirable leadership characteristic. Think of it as "humbition," an amalgam of humility and the ambition Ignatius thought of as doing "more" for the "greater glory of God."

Graduates of Catholic business schools should have antennae that are attuned to the dangers of consumerism, materialism, and individualism. One Jesuit professor I know likes to suggest to students, who are barraged daily with televised, print, or Internet ads that are the infrastructure of our culture of consumerism, that they should ask, "not what this ad invites you to buy; rather ask what this ad presumes you *to be*!" All too often the only honest answer is: "A materialistic, hedonistic, personally insecure consumer, who might also be a sex maniac, given the sex appeal that underlies so many sales pitches!"

We have to encourage our students to think humbition. They need to appreciate the importance of not being possessed by their possessions. Catholic business school educators have a long way to go in persuading their students of the validity and practical worth of the countercultural values that underlie the Gospel. The same values underlie the Catholic colleges and universities that are trying to find their place in the front ranks of American business schools.

27.

Faith-Based Initiatives

Since politics is widely known to be the art of compromise, some religious people were skeptical some years ago about the workability of President George W. Bush's faith-based initiatives. They feared that religious principle will be compromised in the process. That didn't happen, nor need it ever happen.

Others feared that the "establishment" clause (or better, the "nonestablishment" clause) of the First Amendment to our Constitution would be violated if government gave money to religiously motivated organizations to assist them in rendering social services to the needy. This is not a well-grounded fear. Roman Catholicism will not become the established religion of the United States if the federal government funnels federal dollars through Catholic Charities USA in an effort to help the hungry and homeless. Nor will any other denomination become "established" as a controlling religious entity just because that denomination's social service arm is strengthened by an infusion of federal funding.

There is no separation of church and society in the United States, nor was such a separation ever intended by our Founding Fathers. Even though we speak of the "separation of church and state," the wall of separation is a misleading metaphor that appears nowhere in the Constitution. When permitted to function as a wall separating government from any involvement at all with private, faith-based, religiously motivated organizations, the First Amendment is being both misunderstood and misapplied.

There is a time-honored, quite conservative principle in the tradition of Catholic social teaching that should be brought into play in the debate as to whether government money can or should be channeled into religious charities. This principle is intended to keep government in its proper place, active or inactive, depending on the circumstances. It is known as the Principle of Subsidiarity. It applies to any form of organization, not just government. In essence, it states that no decisions or actions should be taken at a higher level of organization that can be taken as efficiently and effectively at a lower lever—closer to the people that will be affected, closer to the ground. The application of this principle depends on circumstances. It forecloses on big government in cases where government would be walking over lower level decision makers to get good things done. Conversely, it would require and fully justify government action in circumstances where programs good for the people should be in place but the resources of lower level organizations fall far short of the need and only government is big enough to make up the difference.

The federal government can fund the Salvation Army's coffee and blankets, but not its hymn books. We're not talking about Lutheran sandwiches or Baptist bandages when we speak of religiously based aid to the poor. We are, indeed, talking about poor people and how society might reach out to them. If faith-related hands are there right now, on the line, at the ready so to speak, why not give them the where-withal to extend themselves in the direction of urgent human need? In examining the list of possible reasons against doing this, don't fail to consider religious discrimination. It is easier to invoke the Constitution than to admit to anti-[fill in the blank] wherever you notice a religion or religious organization that is doing good (not well) and could be doing more (not better), and would be doing more if those who distrust or discriminate against that religion were not so intent in blocking access to the federal faucets.

We didn't hear much about the poor in the first seven years of the Bill Clinton presidency. In my view, it was encouraging some years later to hear about meeting the needs of the poor through nongovernmental agencies that happen to be faith based and are still in close touch with the needy. They know how to reach the poor. The White House Office of Faith-Based and Community Initiatives, established in the first term of the George W. Bush presidency, stood ready to joint venture with them. Some good things began to happen, but apart from the president and his chosen director of the Office of Faith-Based and Community Initiatives, there was little enthusiasm in the White House for this activity then, and not much is evident now.

I keep wondering when critics and skeptics alike will take some time to ask the poor what they think of the idea.

28.

Advice to the Bishops from a Business Executive

I had an interesting exchange a few years ago with a retired business executive, a loyal and practicing Catholic, who has some advice for the hierarchy of the Church he loves. But he has no way of getting through, he said, so he thought I might help by simply putting his thoughts into print.

This gentleman had extensive experience as a senior corporate executive with personal involvement in trade associations. In his view, the root challenges facing the Catholic hierarchy today "are issues of corporate culture, inadequate management training, poor personnel management skills and practices, inadequate financial discipline, and a failure to identify the change in its market or client base, namely, the parishioners."

With respect to the culture—he calls it a corporate or management culture—he looks back to the assumptions "under which our Irish-American Catholic church operated for a century" and finds that they are no longer appropriate. "That modus operandi was premised on a conviction that we Catholics were an embattled minority in this Protestant, secular nation and had to avoid at all costs giving the majority any cause to attack us due to scandal. If problems came up, 'Sweep them under the rug,' and go on." That's how the hierarchy handled the sex-abuse scandal, he says. They are "still operating in the old style, marked by secrecy, command-and-control systems, a monarchial bent, and lack of transparency....They are managing a twenty-first century church with eighteenth-century techniques. We need to kill the old culture and develop a new set of operating assumptions that reflect the realities of the 'market' today. Old cultures die hard; to install a new management system, you must first kill off the old."

In his view, "we do not face a crisis of faith; it is a crisis of management. The basic product is very good; the delivery system is deficient." And he notes, we have a better educated and more thoughtful "client base"—the parishioners.

So where do we go from here? We have a "daunting challenge," he says, "of getting the hierarchical leadership into the classroom." But there is a way.

My correspondent was head of a trade association representing all the brokers and dealers on the New York Stock Exchange at a time when dozens of them failed and many lost money. There was plenty of business, but the so-called back-office crunch due to rising volume had "buried the operations departments in paper and caused any number of firms to fail."

After conducting a series of interviews (and with the help of Marvin Bower's book *The Will to Manage*, McGraw-Hill, 1966), he created "a sequential classic business case about a hypothetical securities firm that underwent all the problems confronting the industry—i.e., an overwhelmed back office, mergers, purchase and sale of branches, inadequate capital to fund growth, as well as personnel and compensation issues." Top executives from member firms were invited, in groups of 20–25, to the Harvard Faculty Club for a three-day seminar, "We had decided," he said, "that they would listen only to their peers." Harvard had nothing to do with the course, but "the venue was important."

"My key point is this," he concluded: "The only ones our church leaders will listen to is each other. Start at the top. Find a way to get the bishops into essentially a self-help management seminar that allows them to identify best practices, identify their own inadequacies in a nonthreatening setting, and develop a common managerial vision."

This sounds like a challenge to a Catholic business school to write the case, provide the venue, and tape the sessions by way of gathering material for a "will-to-manage" textbook that church leadership needed yesterday.

29.
_____

Performance Evaluation in Church Management

Bishop William B. Friend of Shreveport, LA, made a major contribution to a two-day meeting of the National Roundtable on Church Management in June 2006 with an informal auto-biographical account of performance evaluation.

The meeting, held at the Wharton School of Business of the University of Pennsylvania, brought together for the third consecutive year several hundred Catholic business leaders and a handful of bishops, along with dozens of clergy and lay managers of Catholic dioceses and institutions. Under a theme of "Bringing Our Gifts to the Table: Creating Conditions for Financial Health in the Church," participants discussed the applicability of best practices from business to ecclesiastical entities. Early panels explored financial challenges and opportunities, effective diocesan planning, a case study of the financial and structural impact of Hurricane Katrina on the Archdiocese of New Orleans, and the essentials of church financial transparency.

A session was devoted to the "Value of Evaluation in the Church." It featured Charmaine Williams, director of human resources for the Diocese of Fort Worth, and the top executives from two prominent executive search firms—Gerry Roche, senior chairman of Heidrick & Struggles, and Paul Reilly, chairman and CEO of Korn/Ferry International.

Reilly is a "double domer" (bachelor's and master's degrees from Notre Dame, famous for the Golden Dome on its main administration building); Roche a graduate of the Jesuit-run University of Scranton. Both are at the top of their game in business; each is a committed Catholic who wants nothing but the best for his Church.

Paul Reilly explained how what is known in business as 360-degree feedback is used to evaluate executive performance at Korn/Ferry. This involves peer appraisal. If the majority of your management peers say you've got a problem, you've got a problem, not a personality clash or a difference of opinion!

Gerry Roche showed a preference for one-on-one, look-'em-in-the-eye, candid assessment of the strengths and weaknesses of those who report to him. Set clear expectations; then measure progress toward agreed-upon goals next time you sit down together for an evaluation conversation. Unfulfilled potential is the target. It will never get filled absent honest evaluation and clear communication. His essential message: whoever you are, whatever you do, get yourself evaluated!

The subtext for this discussion was how to do this in ecclesiastical circles. Who gives the bishop a performance review? Can a pastor get an honest 360-degree feedback from his peers? Do associates have a chance to contribute to the evaluation? How about parishioners?

Bishop Friend's contribution came during the open-forum discussion following the panel presentation. He had spoken to the group the day before about "exploring financial challenges and opportunities" in the wake of the clergy sex-abuse scandal that rocked the Church in 2002. His credibility and integrity were evident, so it seemed natural for someone in the assembly to ask how he, as bishop, handled his own performance evaluation. His response was both moving and instructive.

Open up to a bishop friend, he said. Select someone you respect and trust, someone who knows both the burdens and benefits of your office. Take time away every now and then. Have with you the set of instructions (the "Directory") you receive from the National Bishops' Conference when you are ordained a bishop. Do a point-by-point reflection together that leads to self-examination as well as peer evaluation.

I would add that this could easily be enlarged to a three-corner conversation. Add a lay friend who is an experienced and trusted manager. There is something very Catholic about a trinitarian model; something wonderful could result for the bishop and those he serves.

PART THREE
_____

Education and Family

30.

Thinking About the Future of Catholic Schools

Where is the future for Catholic schools? It's all out there in front of us, said a group of eighteen committed Catholics who asked me to facilitate their discussion on a pleasant Sunday a year or so ago. They wanted to talk about the future of Catholic education. They are all products of the system of elementary and secondary Catholic education. They continue to support it. Some even participate as teachers and administrators. But it is difficult for them to see clearly the size, shape, and composition of the enterprise twenty years from now.

They were convened by a business executive who wants to see the system succeed. He asked me if they could come from a neighboring state to the campus where I work—St. Joseph's University in Philadelphia, PA—to engage in a one-day retreat for purposes of mutual reinforcement, planning, prayer, and the generation of new ideas.

By sad coincidence, news broke just a few days before we met of the decision of the Philadelphia Archdiocese to close two of its best known high schools: Cardinal Dougherty High School once enrolled 6,000 boys and girls; Northeast Catholic High School for Boys enrolled about 5,000 at its peak. When the decision to close was made, their numbers were 642 and 551, respectively. According to one diocesan planner, the writing (demographics and dollars) was clearly on the wall more than a decade earlier that these two schools, each in an urban working-class neighborhood, were

not going to make it. The closures were announced simulta-
neously with the publication of plans for two new Catholic
high schools in the outer-ring suburbs.

Forget for the moment about the lost opportunity to
evangelize and educate the children—African American, Hispanic, Korean, and Vietnamese—who live near the schools
that would close. Let others discuss the possibility of convert-
ing these facilities into senior housing complexes or Catholic
community centers, if the archdiocese decides to retain ownership and not sell them for commercial development. That's
for others to discuss and decide. My group was looking for
options to save the system in their own small diocese.

Endowment for parochial schools was discussed. Why
could not older parishioner homeowners (particularly wid-
ows and widowers with no dependents) be asked to will their
houses to the parish with the understanding that when they
died, the properties would be sold and the cash received
placed into an endowment for the parish school? Eight
houses thus sold could produce funded "chairs" for each of
the eight classroom teachers in the elementary school.
Principals and counselors could also occupy funded chairs,
which, if not fully "upholstered," could produce income that
would offset a substantial slice of their annual salaries. On
the occasion of the death of any parishioner, memorial contributions could be made to the parish's general education
endowment. We have to be creative in strengthening the
financial infrastructure of our schools.

Participation in the political process could succeed in
putting vouchers in the hands of parents of children in
parochial schools. Teacher tax credits (not to be confused with
tuition tax credits) could provide preferential tax treatment to
any teacher, public or private, thus acknowledging the importance of the work the teacher does in enhancing the productive capacity of the nation's economy. If businesses can receive

investment tax credits, why can't teachers? Their work is an investment in the future.

How about Catholic school consolidation? Why not try an ecumenical cooperative model (cooperate with other religious-purpose schools in nonreligious activities)? Economic cooperation from pre-K through high school could save insurance dollars and trim the purchasing bill for any one school. And so it goes—thinking and planning our way into an unknown future.

31.

Send Your House to School

Is the private Catholic elementary school sustainable in the future? How do we maintain the talent at the front of the classroom? How do we attract and retain outstanding teachers and talented low-income students? Money is an essential part of any answer to these questions.

My suggestion to those who are genuinely concerned about these questions sounds strange, I know, but let me state it and then explain. Send your house to school is my recommendation. As I indicated in the previous essay, we have to find a way of saying this to older homeowners with no mortgage and few or no obligations to family. Their home will eventually and certainly become just a house once again. They'll be gone and the house will remain. It will probably be worth more than it was when originally purchased; its market value will surely be significant.

We need to find a way of explaining to anyone who is so inclined that they can arrange now for their house to go to school—to go quite literally to a private, parish, parochial school—as a gift. Any homeowner can decide now to will that home to a Catholic school. The will can instruct the school to sell the house and put the money from that sale into an endowment that will yield, in perpetuity, funds to pay a teacher's salary or a student's tuition. That is a great way to keep good talent in the front of Catholic school classrooms. The scholarship option will keep Catholic education within reach of low-income children.

Nationwide there are many Catholics who can think now about sending their houses to school. They can make a provision for this in their wills. They could designate the gift to become an endowed chair for a parochial school teacher or administrator, or an endowed scholarship for a child.

The arithmetic is simple. Apply the five-percent formula that typically governs the management of any endowment. For example, if managed properly, a $100,000 endowment can produce an annual income yield of $5,000 in perpetuity. Anything above a five-percent yield can be applied to principal and thus permit the asset base to grow. Moreover, as the value of the asset base grows, the yield on five percent grows accordingly. Suppose the house were worth $1,000,000; what an impact that gift would make every year! Talk about a gift that goes on giving!

The donor can put a family name on the endowment. The named chair or scholarship can honor or memorialize anyone the donor chooses to name. Even more important is the fact that now unknown, even not yet born, children will be the beneficiaries of the donor's thoughtful generosity. Provision can be made when the endowment is established that, in the event the particular school ever ceases to exist, the gift can go to another charitable purpose designated by the donor.

The vexing problem of how to sustain Catholic private education, particularly at the elementary and secondary levels, has a solution that is out there just waiting to be applied. It is hidden away in mortgage-free real estate owned by elderly

Catholics who, for whatever reason, are free of obligations to the next familial generation. There are not all that many of them, but there are enough to make an enormous difference.

They just need to be reminded that when their home becomes once again just a house and they've gone home to heaven, the value of that asset can be put to work in sustaining another valuable asset, private Catholic education, in perpetuity.

32.

Are We About to See a New Era for Catholic Schools?

Scranton Prep was a great all-boys school when I taught there as a Jesuit scholastic from 1956 to 1958. It's still a great school, as the boys I taught were quick to affirm when they returned in 2010 to celebrate the fiftieth anniversary of their graduation and tour a new, modern facility that serves a current co-ed student population of eight hundred.

The class of 1960, now in or near retirement, includes scientists, lawyers, physicians, entrepreneurs, priests, teachers, journalists, and business and government executives. They attended class in a four-story converted hospital with small classes (and classrooms), no auditorium, an outdoor asphalt gym, and, with the exception of a public address system, zero technology.

At the reunion, one member of the class of '60, who is both a PhD physicist and physician, remarked to me, "What Prep really had going for it in our day was great teachers. We didn't need anything else."

This is worth pondering in a nation that is "Waiting for Superman" to solve the problems of its public schools. That's

the title of a film documentary and Web site (WaitingFor
Superman.com) that wants to provide "tools, actions and
resources designed to ensure a great education for every
child in America."

There is no Superman on the way, this film acknowledges, as it praises charter schools and showcases the des-
peration of low-income parents who want better schooling
for their children. The documentary goes over the top in lay-
ing blame at the feet of teachers' unions, but is right on target in demonstrating that great teachers make great schools.

How to attract and retain great teachers is a challenge
for all schools, public and private. How to reward them financially is a challenge awaiting a response from private philan-
thropy and the public purse.

The Archdiocese of New York is facing up to that issue
now. It surprised some and angered others recently with a
plan to shift financial responsibility for parochial schools
from parishes to the 2.5 million Catholics in the Archdiocese.
Those Catholics who have no school-age children and those
parishes that have no schools are being asked to meet their
collective responsibility and support Catholic elementary and
secondary education.

What is going to happen in the public sector is anybody's
guess. Public education has traditionally been a local, not federal responsibility. Real estate taxes traditionally fund local
school districts. When neighborhoods decline and the real-
estate tax base shrinks, the quality of local public education
erodes. Not to mention the negative impact on enrollment of
neighborhood poverty and drug abuse among the young.

Arguably, there is no better social welfare program than
a full-employment economy. If jobs and housing are brought
into proper alignment with the human dignity of every citi-
zen, public schooling will prosper. That's because teaching

positions will be a prominent part of the improved employment picture and good teaching will make better schools.

In the private sector, a sense of vocation and renewed commitment to service will attract talent to the teaching profession. But it will take money—lots of it—in the form of endowment, annual giving, tuition payments, and diocesan subsidies to keep good teachers in Catholic schools, just as it will take courage, accompanied by compassion, to direct poor teachers to other pursuits.

The national debate over educational reform will influence diocesan debates about the future of Catholic elementary and secondary education. Yes, vocations to religious communities that used to staff Catholic schools are down. Yes, the cost of Catholic education is up. Nothing new there. But what might be new is a creative commitment on the part of Catholics—simply because they are Catholic—to save Catholic schools.

33.

Catholic Mission and Identity

There is a lot of conversation these days about Catholic identity in Catholic schools, colleges, and hospitals. I've been interested in that topic over the years because of past involvement in Catholic higher education. But in 2006, I began a two-year interim term as president of my high school alma mater, St. Joseph's Prep in Philadelphia. So I began looking at the mission and identity question through the secondary school lens.

We stated publicly that "the mission of Saint Joseph's Prep as a Catholic, Jesuit, urban, college preparatory school is to develop the minds, hearts, souls, and characters of young men in their pursuit of becoming men for and with others." And we found it useful to engage students, faculty, alumni, trustees and others in spelling out what each of those four defining characteristics meant.

I'll touch on just one of them here—the Catholic marker. By *Catholic* we said we mean that the Prep "is grounded in the person and teachings of Jesus Christ who established a Church that has a tradition, creed, body of doctrine, moral code, and sacramental system that are essential to the life and culture of this school." It is helpful, of course, to say, as that sentence does, what we mean by *Catholic*, but more important to say what we do because we are Catholic. Here are five *quia clauses* (*quia* is the Latin word for "because") that spell out the educational consequences of our Catholic commitment and these are included in the mission statement of the school.

- Because we are Catholic, we strive for a personal relationship of friendship with Jesus Christ so that we may, in the words of St. Ignatius Loyola, founder of the Jesuit order that sponsors this school, "love him more intensely and follow him more closely."

- Because we are Catholic, "instruction and formation in religion, rooted in both Scripture and Tradition, cover Catholic faith and morals while opening the minds of students to an ecumenical outlook and an appreciation of, and respect for, other faith traditions."

- Because we are Catholic, "we foster in students a consciousness of their shared sonship under God and their brotherhood with men and women of all races, nations, and cultures of the world."

- Because we are Catholic, "we instruct our students in their responsibilities as stewards of God's creation. And because we are Catholic, it is our aim to form leaders—men of competence, con-

science, and compassionate commitment—who
choose to order their lives in a radical way toward
God, as modeled for us by Jesus Christ in love and
service to others, all for the greater glory of God."

Similarly, the mission statement makes plain what it
means by Jesuit, urban, and college preparatory, and goes
on to spell out the consequences for the school of each of
those defining attributes. The entire statement is available
at www.sjprep.org.

By specifying the aim to educate "men for and with
others" (it is an all-boys school), the school community
incorporates into its mission statement the words of the late
superior general of the Jesuit Order, Father Pedro Arrupe,
who said in 1973, "Today our prime educational objective
must be to form men for others." Father Arrupe's successor,
Father Peter Hans Kolvenbach, introduced the notion of
"men with" as well as "for" others in order to make the point
that those moved by Ignatian spirituality are in solidarity
with those they help and can learn from them.

It is a healthy exercise for any institution to state its
mission and then face up to the challenge of pursuing the
implications of what that statement says. Not to do so, publicly and in print, is a sign of fear and failed leadership.

34.
_____

Think About the "isms" in Your Life

Everyone can remember being introduced to prefixes and
suffixes in grammar school. That's the kind of thing "grammar" school is supposed to do. It was fascinating to see how
a prefix shifted the direction of a word, and how a suffix
gave it a special emphasis or tilt.

Take, for example, the Latin root of the English word for fold, *plic* (the verb would be *plicare*) and notice what different prefixes can do to its meaning: explicate, replicate, duplicate, implicate. Similarly, the word *unite* gets a massage at the hands of different prefixes: reunite, disunite.

And consider how the suffix "ism" has a way of throwing a noun into italics or boldface print. It introduces a bias, a tilt, an imbalance. Terrorism has been on everyone's lips since September 11, 2001. Even without the help of a suffix, *terror* grabs your attention and makes you think. Add an "ism" to that dread word and you can almost feel the shivers working their way up your spine. Put the prefix "bio" in front of *terrorism*, and wait for your stomach to start churning.

We've been working to eliminate, or at least contain, racism, sexism, consumerism, and materialism in society. We were happy to see what we welcomed as the collapse of Communism in 1989. Capitalism has its excesses that we want to check in order to keep markets and people really free. Individuals are great to have around (we couldn't stay sane without them), but individualism is an aberration that makes living together difficult.

You can run out your own list of additional "isms" and reflect on how they affect you, your family, and the world in which you live. Atheism, Socialism, militarism, pacifism, patriotism, globalism, isolationism, Liberalism, Conservatism. Fans congregate in ballparks, but fanaticism has no place there. Commercial activity keeps the wheels of the economy turning, but commercialism kills the spirit.

What, then, about Catholicism? Does that word connote a bias or convey an undesirable imbalance? Are we Catholics partial, if so, to what? Do we overemphasize anything or assume too much when we speak of our Catholicism?

I would argue that Catholicism is the one tolerable "**ism**" that cannot be carried to excess if we let that little suffix make the following point: We are lowercase "c" catholic in our outlook. We find God in all things. We are worldwide in our love. That assertion is, of course, easier made that achieved. If we were put on trial for our universalism, our knowledge and love of all, where would the verdict come down? Knowledge has to come before love. Many Catholics are insufficiently catholic in their knowledge of other faiths, languages, and cultures. We've been forced to think about that in the wake of September 11, 2001; we should take the time to do some catch-up studying.

Knowledge and love first, unity later. That path has to be taken if we are to be part of the answer, as God surely wants us to be, to our High Priest's prayer, "that they may be one" (John 17:11).

"If you're looking for the key to the universe," wrote a young friend to me not long ago, "I've got some good news and some bad news for you. The bad news is, there is no key. The good news: The universe has never been locked."

To which the humble might reply, I hope we Catholics can say the same.

35.

Lesson for the Young: There Is Strength in Gentleness

On West Street at the edge of Shenandoah, PA, there's an empty lot with a permanent marker that reads: "Site of the Birthplace and Boyhood Home of Walter J. Ciszek, SJ." Jesuit Father Walter Ciszek's book *With God in Russia* (with Daniel L. Flaherty, SJ, McGraw-Hill, 1964) recounts the story of his growing up in Shenandoah; his leaving town in 1928, against his coal-miner father's will, to join the Jesuits;

his postordination assignment to the "Russian Missions"; and his twenty-three years in Soviet prisons and labor camps for the crime of being a "Vatican spy."

My mother grew up just a few blocks from Wally Ciszek's birthplace. Her father was the town's general physician and surgeon. He delivered most of the babies and attended, my mother once told me, to the victims of violence in the days of the Molly Maguire labor uprisings in the coalfields. Her family home on Main Street, which housed my grandfather's office, was, like the Ciszek home, eventually razed. There is no historic marker there, just a gas station and convenience store.

I have many memories of childhood visits to Shenandoah. Sunday morning bells called worshippers to the Irish church (the official Catholic diocesan parish), the Lithuanian church, the Italian church, the Polish church, and several onion-dome Greek churches. There were a few Protestant churches in town and a synagogue too.

The "Pool," a weekly lottery, brought everyone into town on lively Saturday nights. Some residents called the borough "little New York." Located midway between Scranton and Harrisburg, Shenandoah had a population of about 25,000 when anthracite was king; it's down to about 5,600 now. Hispanics, mostly Mexicans, attracted by factory work and farm labor opportunities, have added to the ethnic mix.

I have memories of seeing tough little Polish kids like Wally Ciszek (whom I didn't know then but met many years later) smoking cigars. One of my cousins, Tom Coakley, an Irish kid, played football for Shenandoah High. I had the impression from him that the gridiron surface was more coal slag than grass. They were all tough kids.

Sadly, Shenandoah made disturbing national news several years ago. Luis Ramirez, 25, an illegal Mexican immigrant, died from head injuries and a severe beating at the hands of several teenage boys, all Shenandoah High School football players. They were of Slovak, Irish, Lithuanian, and Polish extraction. Their motive, according to the *New York Times*, was not immediately clear, but ethnic tensions and hatred, fueled by alcohol, appear to be the cause. Two were later convicted of murder in federal court and sent to prison.

Many of my relatives are buried in the Annunciation Cemetery in Shenandoah Heights, overlooking the town. I visit there once or twice a year. I have no living relatives in town now so when I return, I typically see familiar places but no one that I know. The ethnic mix is nothing new; the hatred, however, is.

Ironically, in that summer of ethnic violence in a tiny town connected to the rest of the world by television, *South Pacific* reopened on Broadway with a good deal of fanfare after a fifty-year absence. Shenandoahans undoubtedly heard about it. I hope they also heard again (or perhaps for the first time) the line from the song "You've Got To Be Carefully Taught" from that show that reminds us, "You've got to be taught to hate."

Who taught these Shenandoah teenagers to hate?

And as high school football, rugby, lacrosse, basketball, and other sports get up and running each year all over the country, who's going to convince the athletes that they can play tough, but never dirty; that strength is good, but violence bad; that life within the rules is the good life, and that success on the playing field must never yield to arrogance and vicious behavior on the streets?

We have to demonstrate to our young the wisdom of strength-in-gentleness, and teach them there is no place for hatred in their lives.

36.

_____

For Parents, www Need
Not Mean Worldwide Worry

In the fall of 2002, the *New York Times* reported that "Family Guidance Can Blunt the Effect of Video Violence." Under that headline, the paper noted:

> In their house in Yellow Springs, Ohio, Will Lapedes and his parents were negotiating a conflict over electronic turf. Will, 14, wanted a computer in his room. For his parents, this raised a red flag. "We wanted to be able to see the screen," his mother, Maureen Lynch, said. So they compromised, putting the machine in the hallway outside his room. From this roost, he chats online, looks at sports Web sites and plays an array of video games. Most of them, he said, are "pretty gory."

What's the issue here? Why is Will's mother concerned? What might Will be up to on the Web? Or worse, what might some not-so-nice people be up to out there in cyberspace? Some are setting traps for Will and his brothers, sisters, and neighborhood pals (and the neighborhood, by the way, thanks to the new technology, is now not just around the corner but around the world).

Why are parents worried not only about the Internet, but also about video games, tapes, films, and all sorts of things that are finding their way into the minds of the wide-eyed young through the ubiquitous screens and monitors that attract young eyes much in the way that moths are drawn to flame? Talk about not talking to strangers! Parents now have worldwide worries in this new dot-com day that dawned not all that long ago.

Parents will always have the problem of figuring out where trust ends and neglect begins in the matter of supervising their youngsters. Curious, isn't it, that the computer screen unit is called a monitor and the issue bothering Will Lapedes' mother in the news story just cited deals with monitoring what Will is doing in front of a monitor! The compromise agreement is a transparency or sunshine solution so often applied to business, political, and professional ethics questions: Keep it out in the open, in the hallway where all can see what's on the screen. (But what happens when the portable laptop or the smart phone finally displaces the more stationary PC?)

Although parents should indeed monitor, be on the alert, and attend to their supervisory responsibilities, all of us should think about confronting what concerns us in this area, namely, sex and violence, with workable alternatives. What if love and courage were to displace sex and violence in the entertainment media? What if we substitute creativity for censorship, and what if we take whatever steps we can to stimulate the production of stories, films, plays, games, and entertaining images that portray genuine courage (not mindless violence) and genuine love (not exploitative, sensationalized sex)?

The nation has to become more interested in creativity—the creative arts, writing, advertising and marketing, and indeed thinking about the integration of both love and courage into our entertainment media.

Why can't love and courage displace sex and violence in the creative imaginations of those who produce the fare that feeds the minds of moviegoers and Internet surfers? Money is a very large part of the answer to that question. Follow the dollar trail to pick up a few more clues. Dollars paid for products of the imagination are, for the most part, traceable to bookstore, online subscription, magazine, and box-office sales, and to advertising revenue derived from anticipated sales to consumers. Many clearly want sex and violence; most do not. And those who don't cannot be dismissed as repressed, rigid, or religious zealots. More often than not, they are balanced human beings who, as children, heard and read good stories, learned to love good literature in their formal education, and maintained a reading habit for the rest of their lives. Now all they have to do is outspend the bad guys in the entertainment market and hope their dollar votes will reawaken creative expressions of love and courage.

Censorship is not the answer. Attractive, creative programming is. Denunciation of inferior fare will never be an effective substitute for positive steps taken to encourage and reward creativity.

37.

A Question of Character

There seems to be no effective technical solution to the societal challenge of protecting children from pornography on the Internet. Anyone interested in applying appropriate safeguards will have to look to character development in the young for a genuine solution.

There are various screening and blocking devices that parents, school districts, and libraries can employ and—to address a concern of public schools and public libraries— are also constitutionally permissible. There are, however, ways to get around the blocks and slip through the screens. Kids will find those ways and use them if they so choose. Hence the issue reduces to the exercise of freedom, and the question becomes one of the strength of character behind those free (and often unaided) choices.

Never assume that anyone's character, let alone the character of a child, is fully formed. By definition, no child is yet mature. No maturing child is immune to temptation. No curious child is safe from the cyberspace equivalents of touching the hot stove, tumbling into the unprotected swimming pool, talking to strangers, and getting into any "nice man's" car.

Children need supervision and love. Parents and teachers provide both. Children need adult reference points. Adults are there to answer questions and point inquiring minds in the direction of right (i.e., in the sense of sensible, ethical, correct, and age-appropriate) answers. Experimentation is part of the discovery process; reckless endangerment is not.

One of the subtitles of Stephen Covey's famous bestselling series, *The Seven Habits of Highly Effective People* (Simon & Schuster, 1989), is *Restoring the Character Ethic.* Restoration of the character ethic in the development of the young in America is a central part of any strategy that might be employed to protect children from pornography on the Internet. What might this entail?

Character lies within. Covey's "habits" are in fact principles. They are internalized values or convictions that work from within to prompt external actions. Once internalized they become habitual—they are habits; they facilitate habitual behavior. The strategy needed to protect children in the matter of Internet pornography must outline guiding principles that can be freely chosen by the young and, once internalized, serve to prompt appropriate behavior. A person of character is a principled person. Significant adults—parents, teachers, coaches, counselors, clergy—articulate and explain principles to the young. It is up to the young to assimilate them.

Encouraging youngsters to become principled persons is no easy task. Both faith and reason have a role in this. Faith-based principles and religiously grounded values can be internalized in the developmental process. They need never conflict with reason. They can serve to help a child judge what is or is not reasonable in a context broader than the immediacy of pleasure and pain, of getting caught or getting away with it.

Every parent has the difficult task of determining where trust ends and neglect begins. They want to trust their children, and their children—particularly in the teen years—want to be trusted. But parents surely don't want to be negligent, and their offspring often find it difficult to appreciate the tug-of-war within a parent's heart between the desire to trust and the fear of neglect.

In the matter of saying no to pornography, as in so many other areas of human behavior, society's best hope for a better future lies with the children. Their elders, however, have the present responsibility of helping, not hindering the young along a safe path to mature character development. A book by Michael Koehler, *Coaching Character at Home* (Ave Maria Press, 2003), might help to get that process going.

38.

House Blessing: Blessed by the Breath of God

I was just passing through on a vacation stopover with old friends in their new beachfront home on the New Jersey shore when they asked me to bless the house. No ritual or holy water were at hand. We simply recalled the story of Zacchaeus (Luke 19:3–5), who

> ...was trying to see who Jesus was, but on account of the crowd he could not, because he was short in stature. So he ran ahead and climbed a sycamore tree to see him, because he was going to pass that way.

When Jesus came to the place, he looked up and said to him, "Zacchaeus, hurry and come down; for I must stay at your house today."

Any house blessing can be an invitation to Jesus to visit the place, to protect and sustain it, to hold its inhabitants in peace and safety. Zacchaeus, Luke's Gospel tells us, came down quickly and received him with joy. The presence of Jesus is a blessing in itself; joy in the household is a sign of the continuing reality of that blessing.

Since in this particular place, the sea breeze, like the "breath of God," could be expected to touch this beachfront home every day, we took the following hymn from the Liturgy of the Hours for "Daytime Prayer at Midmorning" and prayed:

Breathe on me, breath of God,
Fill me with life anew,
That I may love the things you love,
And do what you would do.
Breathe on me, breath of God,
Until my heart is pure,
Until with you I will one will,
To do and to endure.
Breathe on me, breath of God,
My will to yours incline,
Until this selfish part of me
Glows with your fire divine.
Breathe on me, breath of God,
So I shall never die,
But live with you the perfect life
of your eternity.

(Music: H. E. Wooldridge, 1845–1917;
Text: Edwin Hatch, 1835–89)

And then in the name of this husband and wife, owners of the house, whose hospitality would welcome their children and grandchildren, as well as countless friends to this vacation home, I prayed, "Lord, may the breezes that pass around and through this house serve to remind us of your gentle touch and protective presence. Keep all who dwell here in your grace. Protect and preserve this place from all danger. May the breath of God be felt in the breeze moving through this house as a sign of your powerful presence and unfailing love. Amen."

Thinking of Christ as presence and power—present to Zacchaeus ("for I must stay at your house today") and powerful enough to sustain in existence all of creation, therefore powerful enough to protect all persons and all homes from evil and injury—I also had to think of some of the frightening dimensions of seashore reality: hurricanes and lightening strikes, accidents happen, houses burn, people drown. Even though an all-powerful God is present, accidents and injuries can still occur.

Figure that out as you walk the beach! Ponder it as you enjoy a sunrise or sunset at the shore when the gentle breeze reminds you of the breath of God. What about the times, certain to come, when the breeze gives way to wind and the winds rise up to hurricane force? Divine power and presence are still there, but what about divine protection?

That's where faith comes in, faith that carries you through the fourth stanza of that breviary hymn: "Breathe on me, breath of God,/So I shall never die." All you can do is say Amen to that and put your faith in the infinite ocean of God's protective love.

39.
_____

Faith, State, and Fatherhood

This could be considered a Father's Day story, but it's worth telling at any time of the year. Former Pennsylvania Governor and U.S. Attorney General Dick Thornburgh was the dinner speaker at Princeton Theological Seminary during a seminar on "Faith, Ethics and the Law." Panel discussions earlier in the day encouraged participants, mostly lawyers, to reflect on the relevance of their religious faith to a variety of ethical challenges in life and law. Thornburgh's speech was titled "The Role of Faith in Decision Making." His approach was personal. His thoughts were influenced by the launch that evening of his autobiography, *Where the Evidence Leads* (University of Pittsburgh Press, 2003). Written originally as a narrative to be shared with his children and grandchildren, the writer received encouragement to publish it for a broader audience. Many will be glad he did. Politically, he had to deal with the Three Mile Island disaster in his first year as Pennsylvania's governor. He commented how much his faith had influenced his decision making in that unprecedented moment of crisis.

Personally, he had, at age twenty-eight, to deal with the death of his twenty-six-year-old wife Ginny in an automobile crash, minutes after she and their three young sons had delivered their dad to his downtown Pittsburgh law office for what would otherwise have been an ordinary day's work. The boys were not yet school age; the youngest, Peter, was just four months old. The two older boys, John and David, survived the crash without serious injury; Peter, who suffered multiple skull fractures, nearly died. Faith kept this family together.

Thornburgh spoke movingly of Peter that evening at Princeton and spoke with gratitude to God for Ginny Judson, who, three years after that tragic day in 1960, became the second Ginny Thornburgh. The boys had a new mother; she formally adopted them one year later. Not long after that, she and Thornburgh presented the boys with their new baby brother Bill.

Peter, whose mental capacity remains limited as a result of the brain trauma he suffered in the accident, became, said Thornburgh, "the conscience of the family, somehow bringing out our very best. Through him we learned to be more tolerant and appreciative of diversity and more committed to the general welfare of persons with disabilities."

When his parents moved into the governor's mansion in Harrisburg, Peter, age nineteen, and his other brothers moved in with them. Dick and Ginny soon noticed that the attentive house staff and the friendly and ever-present state troopers, there to provide security and transportation, were doing so much for the likable Peter that his self-reliance skills began to erode and the household chores that had served to build up his self-esteem were disappearing.

Trusting in God, they decided it would be best to move Peter into supervised living in a nearby group home where he would share common facilities with other clients and participate in some kind of protected workshop employment.

Peter, now middle-aged, tells people that he "works for the poor," a reference to his regular volunteer service at the Community Food Bank in Harrisburg. Occasionally he spends weekends with his parents in Washington. And that brings me to the point of the story: Father and son spent time together one Saturday at the Washington Zoo. At the end of the day, Dick, with elephants, tigers and giraffes in mind, asked Peter, "What did you like best?" Peter looked at his dad and said, "Being with you."

40.

_____

Praying with Children

Talking to children about God begins in infancy and develops through stages marked notably by mealtime and bedtime prayers. There is a sense of wonder associated with a child's idea of God.

Memorization of prayers is helpful for children. Very early on, children tend to hold hands and recite or sing prayerful words together. This is a point where a parent or teacher can encourage children to imagine themselves as so many links in a hand-holding ring that reaches around the world. An unseen God can be imagined to be somehow, somewhere at the center of the circle—looking out, listening, smiling. The hand being held on either side can be imagined by a given child as a small hand, big hand, young hand, old hand, black, white, or yellow hand, the hand of a soldiers or sailor, the hand of a farmer or factory worker, the hand of an athlete or movie star. Anyone at all who can be presumed to be open to God, can be imagined by the child to be present in the circle.

An atlas of the world in the lap of an adult can be used as a prayer book for page-turning children. Their minds can be stretched along lines of global consciousness and their hearts are opened in gratitude to the Creator of the world. They can be encouraged to pray for children less fortunate than they are, and a sense of solidarity with those in distant lands can begin to root itself in their consciousness.

A family photograph album can become a prayer book, as can a school yearbook, an address book, a scrapbook, a family tree. Anything that can evoke memories of days past and loved ones who have left this world can stimulate prayerful reflection about their lives, values, loves, dreams, disappointments, achievements, and, most of all, faith.

Words alone are not enough in talking about God or sharing faith-related ideas with young children. Drawing materials have to be at hand. Spoken words or lines on paper can provide surprise responses to the question: "What is God like?"

However God-talk is initiated with children, elders have to be ready to say who and what God is in their own lives as they listen to children speak of God in theirs. "What does God look like?" opens up a specifically Christian avenue of reflection that draws out (literally or figuratively) the implications of the Christian doctrine of the incarnation. Ever so gently, children can be helped to see God suffering in human beings who suffer.

Talking about beautiful things is a great way to point to God as reflected in all things beautiful as well as to suggest that God is at work behind every sunrise and sunset, behind every blooming flower or flying bird. But birds fall and flowers fade; the earth quakes and skies grow dark. So expect questions about evil, illness, war, and natural disasters that are theologically challenging to anyone engaged in an honest exploration of the question of what God is like.

Dialogues with children about spiritual things will produce growth on both sides of the conversation. Pray with your children and you will begin to notice growth in them and also in yourself.

41.

Thoughts on Praying for the Young

They are our hope, our delight, and sometimes the focus of our fears. The young.

Look at your own and you will probably agree that they are old enough to be responsible, if not fully self-reliant. They are young enough to represent a brimming potential for a wonderful life. They are well-informed, but not yet wise. They are daring, but not yet demonstrably courageous. They are on their way!

A 2002 National Academy of Sciences report addressed concerns parents might have about traps that unsuspecting youngsters might encounter on the Internet:

> The years between pre-adolescence and late adolescence are often turbulent times, in which youth struggle to develop their own identities. They are eager to be heard, seen, and taken seriously, but often lack the experience and maturity to make responsible choices consistently. They test boundaries in developing their emerging adult personalities, and they take risks that adults would deem unwise. They are often socially uncertain, and they value peer approval highly. And in pre- and early adolescence, hormonal changes generally stimulate their interest in sexual matters. Because of the intensely personal nature of such matters (both sexual and social), the "at a distance" nature of Internet communication and the anonymity with which one can seek out a great variety of information on the Internet is highly appealing to very social but also sensitive individuals. (Dick Thornburgh and Herbert S. Lin, editors, *Youth, Pornography, and the Internet*, National Academy Press, 2002, p. 115)

Talking with the young is, of course important, and it will always be a challenge. Recognizing the insecurities of the young, their desire to be liked, and their longing to belong in the company of their peers, parents and other elders have to be willing to wait patiently for the chance to get through with an encouraging word, an affirmative hug, a reassuring smile. They should also not forget to pray for the young. Saint Augustine's mother Monica is famous for her "copious prayers and tears" for her errant son, as he said in his *Confessions*, which moved God to lead him to baptism as a young adult.

For my book *Praying With and For Others* (Paulist Press, 2008), I composed a prayer, which many parents tell me they appreciate. Living, as I do, in a Jesuit community (a home for unwed Fathers!), I'm happy to share this prayer with real parents who are searching for the right words to express what they feel in their hearts:

> From their excesses, protect them, Lord.
> From their exuberance, protect them, Lord.
> From their foolish risks, protect them without
>   hemming them in.
> Help them always to help themselves to prepare
>   for their unknown future.
> Hold them in your hands only to release them to
>   fly on high in realizing their potential.
> Fill them with a holy confidence that will displace any
>   unworthy arrogance.
> Encourage them to let go of selfishness in exchange
>   for service.
> Teach them to distinguish lust from love, force from
>   fortitude, pride from simplicity,
> and always to choose the better part.
> Freedom is your gift to them, Lord; happiness
>   is their goal.
> Guide them toward that goal in safety and security.
> Amen.

42.
_____

Thinking About Care for the Elderly

By 2030 there will be about 72 million people in America sixty-five years of age or older; that's roughly twice the number of American elderly than in the year 2000. Attention is being paid to the pressure this will put on Medicaid and Medicare. Attention is also being paid to those elderly who will be able to afford some medical services, but not the cost of long-term care in a nursing home. Some say it is time to build a strong home-based and community-based system of care for those who can afford it as well as for those who cannot. The cost of long-term care systems and supports will be astronomical.

On July 31, 2010, *The Tablet* (of London) editorialized on the issue of home care versus institutional care in these words:

> Part of the problem is the home-help versus residential care dichotomy, as if there were only two possibilities. The contrast between them is stark and painful for those who have to move from one to the other, and the emotional damage is even more significant than the financial. Residential homes are both very expensive and often not very inviting, with a strong tendency to institutionalize residents and strip them of personal dignity. What is needed is a financial structure that facilitates a range of options, including affordable village-type communities designed to give elderly people the best balance between supervision and independence which fully respects their dignity as human beings.

The great tradition of Catholic social teaching is grounded on the Principle of Respect for Human Dignity. This is the cornerstone of Catholic social teaching and the Catholic commit-

100 • One Faith, Many Faithful

ment to the common good. The Church has much to bring to the policy debate that is needed today to address the issues surrounding the way America organizes and finances care for its elderly population. This is a crucial social justice issue.

Values define cultures. The broad American culture does not value the elderly; it is a youth-oriented, production-oriented, consumption-oriented culture of me-first materialism. In America if you "do" nothing—i.e., are retired, elderly, ill, or unemployed—you "are" nothing. Sad, but true.

I haven't heard anyone speak of an "elderculture" in America, although the ranks of the elderly are dramatically increasing. With that increase, is there any noticeable value or cultural trait shared by the elderly themselves? Is the elderculture a culture of hope? It would be interesting to know how many of the elderly buy into (and how many others in our society respect) the view of Robert Browning whose poem "Rabbi Ben Ezra" opens with these lines: "Grow old along with me! The best is yet to be,/The last of life for which the first was made:/Our times are in His hand/Who saith 'A whole I planned,/Youth shows but half; trust God: see all, nor be afraid!'"

Notice the value that is expressed there—hope for the aging. This needs to be more widely shared today among the aging themselves. And, linked with compassion, it needs to be widely shared in the broader culture. Compassion must drive the policy debates related to all dimensions of eldercare—social, emotional, medical, and financial.

Neglect of the elderly is a sure sign of a society in need of help. Moreover, such neglect is morally wrong, a social injustice. When we neglect the elderly, we are walking all over human dignity, injuring the common good, and, as a society, totally oblivious to the damage we are doing. It is late, but not too late, to give some thought—Catholic social thought—to care for the elderly.

PART FOUR

People and Ideas

43.

"The Man Who Fed the World"

Norman Borlaug, who died at age 95 in September 2009, is sometimes referred to as "the man who fed the world."

Borlaug is said to have saved more lives than anyone who has ever lived.

He grew up on a farm and received his early education in a one-room schoolhouse in Cresco, IA. As a boy, he wondered why plants and grass grew better in some places than others. His boyhood curiosity led him eventually to pursue graduate studies in plant science and a career that helped teach the world how to feed itself.

Borlaug's contribution came by way of the power of intellect. He developed disease-resistant varieties of wheat and was responsible for major productivity advances in plant breeding. His work led to stunning increases in food production in Latin America and Asia, thus averting mass famines in the 1960s and '70s. Because of him, food-deficit nations like Mexico and India became self-sufficient in producing cereal grains. He won the Nobel Peace prize in 1970. In conferring that award, the Nobel Committee expressed the hope that the provision of bread for a hungry world will also help to assure world peace.

To the extent that we live in a world that is broken by unshared bread, the connection between bread and peace was surely worthy of recognition. That link needs to be remembered now by scientists and statesmen alike, as does the link between the life of the mind and the solution of other major problems confronting humankind.

Tomorrow's research scientists and political leaders are sitting in elementary school classrooms today. Someone has to encourage them to cultivate a sense of wonder, apply themselves faithfully to their schoolwork, and commit themselves to the task of engaging their intellects with the major problems of their times.

I'd love to see "Borlaug" become a verb that means connecting intellectual curiosity with a commitment to the common good. If we're lucky, young people will "borlaug" their way to academic achievement. "Borlauging" might come to mean an exercise of creative imagination in purposeful engagement with challenging problems. There will, I hope, be Borlaug research centers and institutes around the country, perhaps at the University of Minnesota where he studied or Texas A&M where he worked until shortly before he died.

I hope even more that the Borlaug spirit of inquiry and service will find its way into the psyche of many young Americans, the area between their brain and heart. From there, great things can emerge that will provide a lasting tribute to this great man. We literally cannot afford to forget him. And we have to find a way to motivate our young to want to be like him.

44.

Speaking Up on Behalf of the Hungry Poor

I was present at the creation of Bread for the World (BFW), a Christian citizens' lobby founded by Lutheran pastor Arthur Simon is 1974. Art recruited me first to participate in a small advisory group that helped him shape the idea, and then as a member of the board of directors of the resulting organization that now has a membership of over sixty thousand and has, over the years, made a major impact on behalf of the hungry poor on U.S. policies aimed at alleviating hunger at home and abroad.

I was also present when BFW celebrated its thirty-fifth birthday at a reception and dinner in a Washington hotel, followed by a day of lobbying on Capitol Hill for improved foreign aid. This happened as the global financial meltdown, along with war, drought, political instability, high food prices, and widespread poverty had pushed, by United Nations estimates, one billion people into the ranks of the hungry poor. These are people who consume fewer than 1,800 calories a day.

The BFW birthday party also marked the launch of Art Simon's memoir *The Rising of Bread for the World: An Outcry of Citizens Against Hunger* (Paulist Press, 2009). The book tells the story of BFW's origins and record of achievement. The "outcry of citizens" in the halls of Congress is a direct response to the outcry of hungry people around the world.

Art Simon is a good listener. You have to be if you are responsible for organizing people around an issue. Hunger is the policy canopy under which BFW thinks and acts. In his memoir, Simon writes,

> Not long after Bread for the World was up and running, we began developing criteria to guide us in the selection of issues and give us a consistent frame of reference against which to test possibilities. These criteria compel us to ask, among other things: Is a proposed target clearly a hunger issue? If it becomes U.S. policy, what difference might it be expected to make for hungry people? Is it an issue that the membership has been prepared to act on? Is it one that can be explained clearly? Would Bread's role be apt to make a significant

difference in the outcome? Questions such as these guide us.

And he adds that once an issue is selected, "focus is essential." Indeed focus is essential and, over the years, Art Simon proved himself to be a focused listener. He is a great example of a servant leader.

By raising a calm, well-informed, and persistent voice at points of power in the U.S. Congress and Executive Branch, BFW is credited with strengthening our national nutrition programs. It is responsible for establishing and funding the Child Survival account in our foreign aid program that has helped reduce child mortality rates worldwide. BFW helped to pass the Africa: Seeds of Hope Act of 1998 to redirect U.S. resources toward small-scale farmers and struggling rural communities in Africa. BFW also led an effort to provide debt relief to the world's poorest countries and tie debt relief to poverty reduction.

There is much more on the record of achievement of this Christian citizens' movement. It all began in the mind and heart of one committed Christian. It continues through the ongoing commitment of thousands of like-minded citizens who are BFW members using their citizenship to help the poor.

45.

Father Ted Hesburgh

When Holy Cross Father Theodore M. Hesburgh, who was born in 1917, turned 91, Stephen Joel Trachtenberg, president emeritus of George Washington University, greeted him by saying, "Father Ted, I hope you're going to live forever!" The president emeritus of Notre Dame replied, "Steve, I already have!"

A *Wall Street Journal* interviewer once asked him, "You've known a lot of leaders. What qualities do the best ones possess?" Father Hesburgh said, "First they have to have intelligence, because leadership has to do with ideas, to be able to see the problems and see solutions to problems. Then, the kind of dedication to not just live your own narrow little life with its narrow interests, but to be willing to contribute something to the commonweal" (*Wall Street Journal*, Sept. 30, 2008).

I remember well the first time I met him. It was in Saint Louis in early 1974 at the Chase Park Plaza Hotel at a meeting of what was then known as the Higher Education Department of the National Catholic Educational Association. I was dean of arts and sciences at Loyola of New Orleans and had just published a back-page "Point of View" article in the *Chronicle of Higher Education*. Ted Hesburgh read the article that day on his flight from South Bend to St. Louis and went out of his way to seek me out and offer a word of appreciation. That pleased me, of course, and also taught me a valuable lesson: never hesitate to offer subordinates and relative unknowns a word of encouragement—not flattery, just genuine appreciation.

Another lesson I learned from Ted Hesburgh was given in a hotel auditorium full of university presidents in New Orleans in 1976 at a meeting of the American Council on Education. The theme of the meeting was "Leadership in Higher Education." Ted, then in the twenty-fifth year of his presidency at Notre Dame, spoke as something of an elder statesman; his topic was "The Presidency: A Personalist Manifesto." He had an attentive and admiring audience, all leaders in American higher education. I was more than casually interested because I was then in my first year as president at the University of Scranton. What I remember most from that talk are the closing words Ted Hesburgh spoke to his presidential colleagues:

I would like to close on a very personal note which I trust you will indulge me. Over the years, I have stood at the graveside of many of my university colleagues and have contemplated the quiet nobility of their lives, so totally and unselfishly given to the higher education of young men and women. Some day, some of my life-long associates will stand at my graveside. At that time, I would feel greatly honored if they will say, Well, we worked together for a long time. We didn't always agree, but that never bothered our friendship or our forward march. At least, he was fair and tried to make the place better. Now he can rest in peace.

I'm not anxious for that day to come soon, but when it does, I would settle for those final sentiments. Who among us would ask for more? The respect of our colleagues is quite enough, assuming God's blessing, too. We won't get the one without the other.

Happily, Father Hesburgh, who was then only 59, is alive and well and, as I write, living in retirement as the oldest member of the Holy Cross Community at Notre Dame. This great priest and educational leader writes to me occasionally; he never fails to sign his letters, "Devotedly in Notre Dame." That devotion both explains and defines his life.

46.

Monk's Tale: A Window on a Catholic World That Is No More

The University of Notre Dame Press released in 2009 *Monk's Tale*, the first of a three-volume memoir by Edward A.

(Monk) Malloy, a Holy Cross priest who served as president of Notre Dame from 1987 to 2005. The narrative opens in 1941, the year of his birth, when "the pilgrimage begins." This portion of the tale runs through 1975, the year Father Malloy received his doctorate in Christian ethics from Vanderbilt University.

Subsequent volumes will, presumably, bring the reader into the executive suite beneath the Golden Dome on the Notre Dame campus and follow the president's pilgrimage of servant leadership around the world. There is no more influential position of leadership in Catholic higher education than the presidency of Notre Dame.

What struck me most forcibly about the formative years of Malloy's life were his family's modest economic circumstances, the centrality of their Catholic faith and practice, the importance they attached to education, and the value of sports in the life of a young boy.

Monk's nickname, acquired in childhood, has no connection to aspirations to monastic life. It seems that there was an older boy in the neighborhood, a good athlete nicknamed "Bunky," whom Malloy admired and began calling "Bunk," thus inviting back upon himself "Monk," a nice alliterative match-up with Malloy. This caught on with all the other kids and has stuck for life.

Malloy's father, who had no education beyond high school, was a claims adjustor for the Washington, DC, public transit company. Monk's mother, also with no more than a high school education, worked as a secretary once her son and two daughters did not need her attention at home.

Home was a modest apartment in the Brookland section of northeast Washington, near The Catholic University of America. Mr. Malloy was a member of the Knights of Columbus and an usher at the National Shrine of the Immaculate Conception. The family was active at St. Anthony's parish where the three children attended parochial school and participated in all the devotions, processions, and altar-server opportunities that were so much a part of pre-Vatican II parish life.

Near their home is a recreational area known as "Turkey Thicket," where Monk Malloy reigned as "mayor," an honor related to his prowess on the outdoor basketball courts. After achieving high grades in parochial school, with instruction and encouragement from the Benedictine nuns, this young scholar-athlete enrolled in nearby Archbishop Carroll High School, an archdiocesan high school staffed by Augustinian priests, where he excelled academically and athletically, so much so that he won an athletic scholarship to Notre Dame.

Anyone concerned about the future of priesthood and religious life in America, not to mention the future of Catholic education, should mine this book for inspiration and ideas, as well as a needed sociological perspective on where we American Catholics find ourselves today. The upward social and economic mobility so many of us have enjoyed in the second half of the twentieth century and beyond has had an undeniable dampening effect on interest in and applicants for the vocation that the mayor of Turkey Thicket chose under the influence of a good Catholic family and schooling, the Spartan simplicities of lower middle-income living, the discipline of competitive sports, and the guidance of the Holy Spirit. "We're depriving our kids of deprivation," is how one of my wealthy friends, who once was poor, sees the problem. How right he is!

All of this deserves a closer look on the part of parents and planners concerned about the future of Catholic life in America.

47.

Spotlight on Raymond Baumhart and Business Ethics

Jesuit Father Raymond Baumhart, retired president of Loyola University of Chicago, is regarded by many as the father of modern business ethics. In mid-April 2010, an impressive array of scholars and business leaders gathered at the Union League in downtown Chicago to honor Father Baumhart, then 86, for his scholarly research in business ethics and his long-time service to Loyola.

In 1961 he published a famous article under the title "How Ethical Are Businessmen?" in the *Harvard Business Review*. *Time* magazine gave the article some well-deserved attention with these comments: "What do executives themselves think of the ethical climate of U.S. business these days? The answer, as reported in a soul-baring survey of 1,700 businessmen by the Rev. Raymond C. Baumhart, SJ, a doctoral student at the Harvard Business School: Not much." And *Time* added: "When ethical questions were put to them, Father Baumhart reports in the current *Harvard Business Review*, an overwhelming majority of the executives gave proper answers for themselves but, when asked if they thought the other fellow would follow the same high standards, were profoundly skeptical" (*Time*, July 21, 1961).

The impression I've retained over the years from the Baumhart article (and his later book *An Honest Profit* [Holt, Rinehart & Winston, 1968]), based on his doctoral dissertation) is nicely expressed by a respondent to his questionnaire who wrote: "It is more difficult to know what is right, than to do it."

This problem is still with us. It continues to call for explanation from those experienced in business and also knowledgeable in ethics. Explanation of complicated on-the-ground business reality, coupled with clear articulation of ethical principles, is what we need.

The problems are now more complex and the principles more refined. Think, for instance, of the much more sophisticated understanding we have today of the idea of justice, including social justice, than we had in the 1960s. Think of the renewed interest in values and the prominence of a field of reflection known as virtue ethics. Think also of the development in our understanding of the great tradition of Catholic social thought and its applicability to the world of business.

We've been through a lot in this country in the area of business ethics in recent years. Recall Enron, WorldCom, Tyco, and other famous cases. Think of the economic meltdown that began with the subprime mortgage crisis in 2008 and the later allegations that fraud on the part of Goldman Sachs may have had a lot to do with it.

We keep hearing calls for reestablishment of integrity in corporate life, for transparency and veracity in business. Integrity means living truthfully; veracity means speaking truthfully.

If we could bring ourselves as a nation—in all its individual, personal, familial, and corporate parts—to refuse to tell a lie, there would be a revolutionary advance in business ethics in this new century. Clearly, ethical leadership is needed in the business community today. We need the kind of ethical leadership that Ray Baumhart examined in scholarly fashion and later brought in person to the presidency of Loyola University. In his 1961 *Harvard Business Review* article, Baumhart defined a leader as one "who raises his own standards above the ordinary and is willing to let other people judge him by these raised standards."

The symposium in his honor recognized Father Baumhart's admirable adherence to the highest standards of scholarship and educational management. It would be great if today's leaders in corporations and business schools could reactivate the Baumhart legacy for the advancement of ethics in business.

48.

"The Pain of Unused Answers"

Loyola University New Orleans was the academic home for many years to the Jesuit sociologist of religion Joseph H. Fichter, who died in 1994. In his book, *Organization Man in the Church* (Cambridge: Schenkman, 1974), Father Fichter has a chapter on "Renewal and Responsibility" where he recalls the famous scientist Glenn Seaborg's phrase, "the pain of unused answers," to express the frustration we feel "when we fail to make the fullest and most beneficial use of all the knowledge and resources this incredible age has to offer." That frustration bothers us today in countless areas of church and national life.

Father Fichter came up with three "c's," three words beginning with a "c," to provide handles for using the knowledge and resources we have to make our way into a better future. To alleviate the "pain of [our] unused answers," he suggested trying "communication, collegiality, and co-responsibility." A great statesman like Abraham Lincoln chose what author Doris Kearns Goodwin called a "Team of Rivals" to form his cabinet. What great churchman is ready now to listen, to consult, and to make "communication, collegiality, and co-responsibility" instruments of ecclesiastical leadership?

Take your pick of national problems (recall the ones debated in the last presidential campaign) and review your most recent list of complaints about the Church; then wonder whether better communication, more collegiality, and co-responsibility might contribute some solutions.

Communication has to be two-way and participatory. Collegiality is the characteristic without which you cannot have a national or church community. Co-responsibility means that public officials and church administrators need others (if not us, then who?) to bring the ship of state as well as the bark of Peter through troubled waters.

Think about your share in that responsibility. You won't know if there are open doors and open ears in the corridors of power unless you give communication, collegiality, and co-responsibility a try. Call your pastor; visit your elected representatives.

All of us, leaders and led, have to be accountable to one another. The democracy we call state and the community we call church literally live on trust. If we simply settle for going our separate ways together, all of us will continue to feel "the pain of unused answers." We simply have "to make the fullest and most beneficial use of all the knowledge and resources this incredible age has to offer."

In a book entitled *I'm the Teacher, You're the Student: A Semester in the University Classroom* (University of Pennsylvania Press, 2005), history professor Patrick Allitt of Emory University writes:

> One of the sad things about being a professor is that we rarely see each other doing what we do best. Each professor has more or less complete classroom autonomy, and although there are classroom exchanges now and again, we often go years at a time without seeing

each other at work....It's a pity and sometimes leads professors to underestimate their colleagues.

Those who do college teaching for a living know all about this underestimation. As for the rest of us, regardless of what we do, we probably contribute, as both citizens and communicants, to the national supply of underestimation. Life could become more interesting and livable if we spent some effort learning more about what others actually do in attempting to meet their responsibilities.

During the semester in which the course described in Professor Allitt's book was taught, the author gave an adult education course in his local community. Teaching grown-ups, he remarks, prompts him to notice how young under-graduates take so much for granted. "What many of them never show, except the handful to whom I gave a lot of personal or remedial help, is gratitude."

His adult students say thanks.

Maybe that's what all of us ought to be saying to one another on the way to strengthening our communication, collegiality, and co-responsibility.

49.

Seven Secular Challenges to the Church

Father Val Peter is outspoken, energetic, always thinking, and acutely aware of what's going on in the world. From 1985 to 2005, he was executive director of Father Flanagan's Boys Town in Omaha, NE.

Later renamed Boys and Girls Town, this safe haven for troubled youngsters has provided family-style living, a first class educational experience through high school, and spiritual formation—on the Omaha campus, as well as sites in fourteen other states and the District of Columbia—for thousands of children ages ten to seventeen who are admitted through juvenile courts or social service agencies. Preference goes to those who have no natural or adoptive parents; many have been physically or sexually abused and most have been involved with the courts.

Father Peter now runs a Los Angeles-based national coalition of organizations called Character Counts. An astute observer of life in the church and secular world, Val Peter published a book titled *Seven Secular Challenges Facing 21st Century Catholics* (Paulist Press, 2009). It is well worth reading.

He sees "seven critical areas and challenges where our culture is not enriching, but rather diminishing our lives." These are (1) diminished respect for authority, (2) the widespread belief that one is free to experience everything, (3) cynicism, (4) mistaken ideological beliefs, (5) learned helplessness, (6) anti-intellectualism, and (7) political correctness. "Learned helplessness" is the label Val Peter puts on the conclusion most of us draw, namely, that "there is nothing I can do to make things better." And the "mistaken ideological beliefs" he identifies include totalitarianism, the MTV culture, and terrorism.

Father Peter suggests that the Catholic Church is in possession of an untried remedy to all these problems, namely, Christian idealism. I'd like to let him speak for himself:

> More than anywhere else I have learned the lessons of the long spiritual journey [of reform and renewal that the Church must take] from my years at Boys Town. I have seen thousands and thousands of young people come to us, all of them filled with anger, loneliness, frustration, and the loss of hope, living in a postmodern culture: antiauthoritarian and cynical. They feel free to experience everything. They embrace MTV's ideology.

In some ways they are hopeless victims. These lives are reduced to a single narrow focus: Should I destroy my life (drugs, sex, and alcohol) or go on? Is it worth the effort to swim against the tide of pain and despair, alienation and dysfunctionality? Or shall I curse God and die? Because of their past, they believe that love (even God's love) has to be merited and they are convinced they are unworthy. This is the lie Adam and Eve believed when they hid themselves from God in the garden. Our job is to help them choose life.

Choosing life is not easy for anyone, young or old, who cannot see what the really good life is. I think of the good life as the life that is lived generously in the service of others. That's a fair description of how Val Peter has chosen to live his very productive life. That's why his advice to twenty-first century Catholics on choosing life wisely and well is worth considering.

50.

The Most Pressing Issue of Our Time

A couple of years ago, I spent some time in West Virginia and Wisconsin encouraging Wheeling Jesuit University students and the directors of Catholic Campus Ministry programs for Wisconsin's state and private colleges and universities to talk about what they see as "the most pressing issue" today's collegiate generation will have to deal with over the course of its collective lifetime

Whenever I raise that question, I declare each person in the audience to be the world's leading expert on his or her own opinion. That's all I'm looking for—an opinion. For a student audience, I extend their lease on life out to age 90.

That means they can speculate on the most important issue that is likely to confront them over the next 70 years or so. I tell them that I have a candidate for most pressing issue in mind, but will not disclose it until they name theirs. (I'll mention mine toward the end of this essay.)

I've done this often over the years and find it interesting to see how the menu changes over time. No mention of Communism or totalitarian rule now. Few indications any more that the excesses of Capitalism will do us in. Terrorism is much on the minds of the young these days. So is nuclear war. Globalization is a big item, and it admits of subdivision into interesting parts: migration of jobs off shore, exploitation of workers in developing countries, imbalances in trade, instability in credit markets, and influx of illegal immigrants to the United States.

The environment is on many young minds—global warming; loss of grasslands, croplands, woodlands, and wetlands. Energy and overpopulation always make the list. You'll hear abortion mentioned along with other life issues.

Big business (greed), big unions (abuse of power), and big government (corruption and inefficiency) are major concerns. Small is seen as ever more beautiful in the eyes of the young, but how to make small into something big enough to meet the challenges of the day is a puzzle. Some wonder about crime and violence being a function of the size of human community today. Will we see more as we grow?

Disease is a major concern, especially HIV/AIDS. The revolution in molecular biology as well as the potential offered by gene therapy (a cure for cancer?) come into the discussion.

Racism and sexism are always mentioned, thus enabling me to point out how the suffix "ism" throws a noun into italics or boldface and creates a distortion, an imbalance, not to mention introducing the dimension of injustice into the conversation. Individualism and the decline in morality are always mentioned. Curiously, the erosion of commitment in human relations and the increase in divorce and family instability are not.

Once the "isms" find their way into the conversation, I introduce my candidate for the most pressing issue today's collegiate generation will have to deal with. Materialism is my nominee. I explain that one can use alcohol without abusing it or becoming addicted, thus avoiding alcoholism. Similarly, we all have to use material things and can manage to do that without abuse or dependency. But just as alcoholism means a damaging dependency and addiction to alcohol, materialism means a dependency and an addiction that displaces immaterial considerations in one's life, not the least of these is the acquisition and use of knowledge, not to mention the practice of religion and development of a functioning spirituality.

Knowledge is necessary to come up with solutions—scientific, diplomatic, humanistic, technological—to any problem that makes the list of most pressing issues. And isn't that why students are in college—to gain more knowledge? Materialism can derail that project. Recommitment to the life of the mind is a solution waiting to be tried.

51.

Where Have All the Leaders Gone?

I have a pen-and-pencil holder on my desk that has "The Essence of Leadership" inscribed on its side. Here are the words: "A true leader has the confidence to stand alone, the courage to make tough decisions, and the compassion to listen to the needs of others. He does not set out to be a leader, but becomes one by the quality of his actions and the integrity of his intent. In the end, leaders are much like eagles ...they don't flock, you find them one at a time." There is no attribution of authorship. My effort to track that down led me to the Web site of the Institute of Association Management (www.iofam.co.uk) where slides, including one with the quotation I cited, were posted from a presentation by Susan Sarfati, the association's president and CEO. The quotation was accompanied by a statement that the source of these wise words is anonymous.

Note in that inscription the words confidence, courage, decisions, listen, actions, integrity, and intent. These are seeds ready to sprout up in any understanding of leadership, a reality more easily described than defined.

According to John Gardner, "Leadership is the process of persuasion or example by which an individual (or leadership team) induces a group to pursue objectives held by the leader or shared by the leader and his or her followers" (*On Leadership,* Free Press, 1990). Notice the verb *induces.* Gardner is at pains to point out that leadership must not be confused with status ("in large corporations and government agencies, the top-ranking person may simply be bureaucrat number one"), nor with power ("many people with power are without leadership gifts").

Decades ago, Dwight D. Eisenhower explained that, "the President does not lead by hitting people over the head. Any damn fool can do that....Leadership is by persuasion, education, and patience. It is long, slow, tough work" (quoted in Emmett John Hughes, *Ordeal of Power* [Atheneum, 1963]). Eisenhower often said that leadership is "the art of getting someone else to do something you want done because he wants to do it." Another very helpful way of defining, or at least describing, leadership comes from Robert Greenleaf—"going out ahead to show the way" (*Servant Leadership,* Paulist Press, 2002).

Followership is the ultimate test of leadership. That seems fairly obvious. If you are going to lead, someone has to follow. Hence, my personal definition of leadership is "the art of inducing others to follow." A variant on that would be, "the art of inducing change," because change is really the name of the leadership game.

Leaders have to maximize their power to persuade; without persuasion, leadership simply does not happen. Goal setting is an essential part of leadership. You can't provide leadership unless you have a strong sense of where you want to go. Goals—both long and short term—bring people together, unify them, and motivate them. Goal setting is a constant task of leadership. Articulating and communicating goals to be achieved—near term or out toward the horizon—is an ongoing leadership responsibility in church and state, wherever people are waiting to be led. Where are we going? How are we going to get there? Once there, what are we going to do? Leadership has to answer those questions.

I'm not naming names or pointing fingers as this book goes to press. I'm just waiting to hear some good answers. Meanwhile, for anyone interested, my book, *Next-Generation Leadership: A Toolkit for Those in Their Teens, Twenties & Thirties Who Want to be Successful Leaders* (University of Scranton Press, 2010) offers ideas and examples of leadership that might be worth considering.

52.

An Encouraging Word

Franklin Delano Roosevelt, whom Chief Justice Oliver Wendell Holmes, Jr. once described as possessing a "second-class mind and first-class temperament," loved the words of the old cowboy song, "Home on the Range." Its reference to the open range "where the deer and the antelope play," is followed by words that matched the president's admirable temperament—"where seldom is heard a discouraging word and the skies are not cloudy all day." Encouraging words originate in a positive attitude.

Attitude is essential to leadership. A positive attitude sets a positive course. A positive person, recognizing that leadership is a person and not a position, attracts other persons to join in the enterprise and work together to achieve results.

Successful presidential candidates have to travel a long road to the White House that is littered with negative, discouraging words. Once the election is over, I look for encouraging words to pave the successful candidate's way into the Oval Office and, more important, I want encouraging words to emanate from the White House to the Congress and the nation from day one in any new administration.

FDR told the nation that it had "nothing to fear but fear itself," even though he himself really didn't know how bad things were for the American economy when he was elected in 1932. Any newly elected president would do well to take an early morning stroll through the FDR memorial that graces a seven-acre plot positioned at three o'clock in the Tidal Basin near the Jefferson Memorial (at 12 o'clock) in Washington, DC.

This memorial is made up of four open-air "rooms" corresponding to each of the four terms of the FDR presidency. On the granite walls are carved words Roosevelt used to inspire the nation to work its way out of the Great Depression.

Words are an important tool of leadership. Words alone, of course, are useless, but words embodying creative ideas that reflect careful analysis are useful. Words that substitute blame for analysis are worthless, but well-reasoned words that point toward positive solutions are what we always need. Today, we need remedies for unemployment, protection against inflation, and restoration of trust in all markets, especially credit markets. We need effective protection from terrorism and all enemy attacks. Perhaps we need protection from ourselves in the form of new challenges to sacrifice and community service. We do not need empty promises; just well-conceived and carefully articulated plans.

During any political campaign, the candidates are doing politics. The successful candidate finds him- or herself faced with the daunting task of doing government. Stump speeches during the campaign say remarkably little about the art of government and much too much about the push and shove of politics.

We do government at the national level through cabinet-level departments led by political appointees but staffed by career professionals. The appointees will represent poor choices if they cannot demonstrate that they possess integrity, creativity, competence, and courage. With each new administration, the career professionals have a fresh opportunity to write their next chapter of creative followership in government service.

All of us have to be ready to sacrifice. All of those at the leadership level in government have to be ready to tell us what they really believe is best for the people, instead of telling us what they think we, in our less enlightened moments, want to hear. Needed after any election and at the beginning of a term in office are encouraging, positive words.

53.
_____

A Second Start for the Jesuits?

Jesuit Superior General Adolfo Nicolas raised an interesting question at a meeting in Mexico not long ago with representatives of Jesuit institutions of higher education from all over the world. He asked them to ponder this question: "If Ignatius and his first companions were to start the Society of Jesus again today, would they still take on universities as a ministry of the Society?"

Father Nicolas then asked whether Ignatius and his first companions "would ask their basic question afresh: What are the needs of the church and our world, where are we needed most, and where and how can we serve best?" So he repeated the question this way: "[W]ould running all these universities still be the best way we can respond to the mission of the church and the needs of the world? Or, perhaps, the question should be: What kind of universities, with what emphases and what directions, would we run, if we were refounding the Society of Jesus in today's world?"

He left that question open to be considered by Jesuits and their lay colleagues. In a certain sense, the Jesuits have to answer that question for themselves, but they cannot answer it by themselves. They have to share ownership of both the question and the institutions with their lay colleagues, who far outnumber the Jesuits in those institutions today.

The institutions are going to survive, even prosper, into the unseen future. The extent and style of future Jesuit engagement with the institutions is by no means clear. Their future identity as Jesuit is going to depend on the extent to which lay men and women who work in those colleges and universities are committed to the core values of the Spiritual Exercises of St. Ignatius of Loyola, who founded the order

in 1540. Apart from the values embodied in the Spiritual
Exercises, it's impossible to understand what Jesuit means.
Moreover, it's not enough to know about, or read the book
of the Spiritual Exercises; it is in the experience of the
Exercises that authentic Jesuit values and principles are
assimilated and eventually lived.

If future lay leaders of Jesuit institutions are men and
women of the Exercises, those institutions will be Jesuit.
But Father Nicolas's question still awaits an answer. Given
the needs of the Church and the world today, would
Ignatius and his original band of brothers, if they had it to
do over again, get into the business of running universities?
Would those universities be noticeably different from the
Jesuit universities we know today?

There's a lot that needs fixing in both the Church and
world today, and the university is a tool that can do only so
much. On the problem side, consider what needs to be
fixed: poverty, unemployment, injustice, hunger, disease,
materialism, secularism, greed, hatred, violence, erosion of
commitment, diminished respect for human life, environmental degradation. The list runs on.

Underlying every problem on that list is the need for the
application of intellect in the search for solutions. The Church
is now less influential and less respected in the world of ideas.
This cultural fact has created a need for individual men and
women of faith to establish themselves as intellectual authorities, influential in the production of ideas. That's the business
of universities. There's a good chance that Ignatius would see
the challenge and want to take it on.

Faith-committed men and women of competence and
courage are needed to meet that challenge. The Jesuits have
to take a good look at what their universities are doing today
to see if they are relevant and capable of attracting the talent needed to make a difference.

54.

To Forgive Is Also Human

Forgiveness finds its way in and out of the news with some regularity. Public reports of marital infidelity in high places keep recurring. Is the wronged spouse willing to forgive? The release of the convicted Lockerbie bomber several years ago and the imposition of light sentences in trials, as well as the acquittal of some prominent persons by the courts, all have a way of confronting grieving survivors and law-abiding citizens with the question of forgiveness.

The challenge to forgive is, for most of us, never far away, but we don't deal with it all that well.

Our better judgment, as well as divine revelation, tells us that we should always be ready to forgive. Is there any limit on that, say, seven times? No, "seventy-seven times" is the Christian answer to the question of how often we should forgive (Matt 18:22).

There is a biblical understanding of "remembering" that means simply to make present again, to relive an event. This is rooted in the Hebrew Bible where to forget is to obliterate and to remember is to keep a relationship very much alive. The Lord "forgets" our sins and "remembers" His promises, His covenant, with us. We can be nothing but grateful for that. In the spirit of gratitude, we have no real choice but to forget our grudges.

Since childhood we've heard it said that "to err is human and to forgive divine," and we excuse our refusal to forgive by acknowledging the obvious fact that we are human, not divine. Far less obvious, however, is the fact that we Christians are "divinized" by the grace of the sacraments and are thus not only expected to forgive, but made capable of forgiving and forgetting (obliterating, for all practical purposes) any offense. God stands ready to forgive; how can we refuse to do the same?

National forgiveness is something that we tend not to think about very often, let alone pray for. Personal forgiveness is another story. We pray for that all the time. But we should think about forgiveness writ large. Our nation, like ourselves, stands in need of forgiveness from time to time. When issues of forgiveness emerge in the news, we might give some thought both to giving and receiving forgiveness on a personal and national scale.

A Proclamation for a National Day of Prayer, issued by President Abraham Lincoln in 1863, read in part:

> And insomuch as we know that by His divine law nations, like individuals are subjected to punishments and chastisements in this world, may we not justly fear that the awful calamity of civil war which now desolates the land may be but a punishment inflicted upon us for our presumptuous sins, to the needful end of our national reformation as a whole people? We have grown in numbers, wealth, and power as no other nation has ever grown; but we have forgotten God....It behooves us then, to humble ourselves before the offended Power, to confess our national sins, and to pray for clemency and forgiveness.

We readily admit that nobody's perfect, but we hesitate to admit that our nation can indeed be quite imperfect, morally flawed, and in need of forgiveness. We can all think of a long list of moral flaws not only in ourselves but in our nation, some supported by law and custom, others tolerated by a permissive society. If we are honest and humble, we will acknowledge a national need for God's forgiveness for our excesses, omissions, and wrongful actions.

In considering the dimensions of the forgiveness we all need, we can get a glimpse of the immeasurable dimensions of our forgiving God.

55.

Ethics and Accountability for Catholic Organizations

The National Leadership Roundtable on Church Management has been up and running for about seven years. It is a lay Catholic initiative with clergy participation that meets in late June for two days, originally at the Wharton School of the University of Pennsylvania, later at Georgetown. The third or fourth gathering attracted about 250 Catholic leaders from business and church organizations and produced three small handbooks on best practices in management—one for parishes, another for dioceses, and a third for Catholic nonprofits.

The third booklet is titled "Standards for Excellence: An Ethics and Accountability Code for Catholic Nonprofits." These standards are intended as a model to influence the operations and governance of Catholic organizations. They are based on values like honesty, integrity, fairness, respect, trust, compassion, responsibility, and accountability. Eight guiding principles are provided and fifty-five standards, described as "more detailed performance benchmarks," are listed.

The same eight guiding principles and fifty-five standards are applied in the other two booklets; hence dioceses and parishes as well as all Catholic nonprofits now have an ethics and accountability code for self assessment. To learn more or purchase copies, visit the Roundtable Web site at www.nlrcm.org or write to National Leadership Roundtable on Church Management, 1350 Connecticut Ave., Suite 825, Washington, DC 20036.

"In pursuit of their religious mission," says the Roundtable, "Catholic organizations seek and use temporal goods." The Roundtable's reason for existence is to encourage church management to use temporal goods ethically and efficiently. The eight guiding principles relate to mission and ministry, governing boards, conflicts of interest, human resources (personnel), financial records, open books, fundraising, and participation in the public life of the community.

Each of the eight principles is elaborated in a set of standards. For instance, the mission-and-ministry guideline is spelled out in a call for mission statements, program and organizational evaluation, establishment of a grievance procedure, protection of confidentiality, and it makes this statement that some will fear but most will welcome: "Nonprofits should regularly monitor the satisfaction of program participants/recipients." For parishes that would mean evaluation of homilies and homilists!

The governance guideline spins off standards relating to long- and short-term planning; development of financial and personnel policies; budget approval; attention to the results of an outside audit and the auditors' management letter; and board responsibility in hiring (within parameters set by canon law) and overseeing organizational executives, including the overall compensation structure.

As to board membership and composition, the standards want a commitment to mission, an absence of any conflict of interest, a manageable board size, the establishment of term limits, appropriate diversity, and zero compensation.

Boards should meet at least four times a year, keep minutes, and have written policies. The organizations they oversee should have written personnel policies and procedures covering the basic elements of the employment relationship (e.g., working conditions, compensation, benefits, vacation, sick leave). Written job descriptions and written performance evaluations are specified as belonging on any list of best practices.

The handbook for best practices in parishes substitutes advisory bodies for boards, and lays out standards relating to parish pastoral councils and finance councils.

Under the financial accountability guideline, the standards cover budget approval, timely financial reports, and, where revenues exceed $300,000, an independent certified public accountant should audit the financial reports. Compliance standards look beyond canon law to all applicable federal, state, and local laws.

Fundraising guidelines include the interesting standard that revenues from fundraising efforts and development activities should be "at least three times the amount spent" in the fundraising effort. There is more of interest in each report. Each "ethics and accountability code," is surely worth reading. The Roundtable deserves a vote of thanks for making these booklets available.

56.

Enhancing Customer Satisfaction in the Parish

Parish churches can take a page from the business playbook to make the worship environment more inviting to both parishioners and visitors. All it takes is a bit of planning and not much expense.

Restaurants, retail apparel outlets, and even banks are finding ways to become more warm, inviting and customer friendly. Low prices alone won't do it, nor will personal attention without imagination. But when personal attention is wrapped in a welcoming environment by the use of lights, display, and music, there is a tug on the heart that draws people in and encourages them to return. Businesses—stores, banks, restaurants, client services—are consciously trying to connect with customer emotions. Creative pastoral planning can enable the church to do the same.

Go online to the American Customer Satisfaction Index (ASCI; www.theacsi.org) and you will be welcomed by these words from Professor Claes Fornell of the Ross School of Business at the University of Michigan, founder of ACSI: "As long as repeat business is important, and as long as customers have a chance to go somewhere else, employees must deliver high levels of customer satisfaction for a company to be successful." Substitute "parish staff" for "employees" and "parish" for "company," and you have the makings of a good strategic plan for any parish.

An obvious area calling for some measure of parishioner satisfaction is the homily. It takes a bit of courage to invite homily evaluations from a parish congregation. But it is happening and should become commonplace. A one-page questionnaire, used on a random basis several times a year, can invite a check-mark response on a scale of excellent, good, fair, or poor, relating to content, organization, ease of hearing, length, and timeliness of the homily just delivered at a given Mass.

The form should invite additional comments and respondents should be told that there is no need to sign the sheet. If audibility is a problem, respondents might be asked to indicate where they were sitting when the homily was delivered.

Any service-rendering agency welcomes client or customer feedback. Any company that puts a product on the market wants to know whether it is ringing up positive or negative marks on the customer-satisfaction register. Why would parishes not want to know how their homilies are being received?

A useful mood-setting device for the eucharistic liturgy might be thought of as "lights down; music up." For ten minutes before Mass begins, let the organist play quietly the melodies of the several hymns to be sung during Mass. With lighting dimmed to about half the normal intensity, the music works its way into the consciousness of those who will soon be singing the hymns. A moment before Mass begins, the lights come up and the music for the opening hymn comes in at full volume. The congregation rises and so does the heart-felt expectancy of those whose voices join in the entrance hymn.

With the lights dimmed as the assembly gathers, another device that serves to focus attention and cultivate devotion is a targeted spotlight on specific objects of visual art, not all at once but selectively on the crucifix, tabernacle, altar, statues, stained glass windows, paintings, stations of the cross. This works before Mass and again in the moments after communion. It creates a visual hush. The impression can be preserved, even taken home, by simply making available to all who want one an inexpensive postcard-size reproduction of the artwork.

This sort of thing works in business; it could bring more "business" to the pews. Lots of good ideas are out there just waiting to be tried.

57.

When the Rectory Telephone Rings

Like any business, a parish should want to be customer friendly and readily responsive to telephone inquiries. This means no undue delays in having a call answered, and, if the

call triggers a recorded welcome, there should be a merci-
fully brief menu of press-button options on the way to contact with a live voice at the other end of the line.

Many businesses include response time in the set of
metrics they use in their normal efficiency measures for
meeting customer needs expressed in phone calls. Reduction
in the time a caller has to hold is always desirable. Sometimes
a live voice receives the call, and then one of several actions
(not all customer friendly) follows: (1) "Hang on," is one of
the less elegant instructions; (2) "Please hold," is always better to hear, unless it means being shunted off into soundless
isolation; (3) the "hold" status may be accompanied by soft
music, a tune-in to all-news radio, or recorded advice on the
benefits of exercise—none of which is tolerable for extended
periods of time; or (4) the exasperating experience of having
your request heard but not acknowledged; you are simply
switched to another line that may or may not be related to the
object of your original inquiry. Obviously, this is not a good
way to initiate dialogue or open a transaction in any business
or any parish.

Callers to some parishes automatically get the
recorded Sunday Mass schedule (which can be extensive)
before hearing a live voice or other recorded options. In
some cases, callers hear a live voice identifying the parish,
giving the receptionist's name (often inaudibly), and asking
"How may/can I help you?" when a simple, "Hello, welcome
to St. Malachy's" would do just fine.

When a nationally known business was having problems with the quality of its customer service hotline, one of
its top managers decided to investigate. He learned that as
a result of insufficient training, the customer service representatives were not answering calls promptly.

Here is how a friend described the situation to me:

This caused the caller to be in an irate mood by the time the call was eventually answered, resulting in a confrontational conversation and further dropping the morale of the employees at the call center." So the supervisor decided to "place a mirror in front of each telephone operator and beseeched them to look into the mirror before and during the call. He asked them to make sure that their facial expressions were friendly. It was a simple move, but it achieved the desired result.

If every pastor put a mirror in front of each rectory phone (including his own) what wonders might be worked in the cultivation of improved parish relations!

Try it and see. Put a mirror in front of you as you speak on the telephone and notice how the sound of your voice changes for the better when you smile. Speaking through your smile is just another way of providing "service with a smile" and that, of course, should be standard operating procedure in parishes trying to extend the ministry of the one who "came not to be served but to serve, and to give his life [as] a ransom for many" (Mark 10:45).

58.

Who's Conducting the Exit Interviews?

Ever since Larry Bossidy, former CEO of Allied Signal and the Honeywell Corporation, raised the question, I've been giving it a lot of thought. Bossidy—a devout Catholic whose best-selling book *Execution* (Random House, 2002), which is co-authored with Ram Charan, and, as Bossidy likes to say, is about effective management in business, not capital punishment—addressed a meeting of the National Leadership

Roundtable on Church Management in 2008 and mentioned this good idea. He pointed out that if a business were losing customers at the rate the Catholic Church in the United States is losing members, someone would surely be conducting exit interviews. Immigration, largely Hispanic, is shoring up the aggregate numbers, but there's been a dramatic decline in Sunday Mass attendance and church life among American-born Catholics.

Does anyone know why? There are several obstacles to finding out. First, pastors and bishops tend not to think like business executives, so conducting exit interviews is not likely to occur to them. Second, no one is sure how to reach those who are no longer in the pews. And third, we really don't know what to ask.

Assuming that we find a way to connect, here is a set of questions that might be asked:

- Why have you stopped attending Sunday Mass regularly?
- Are there any changes your parish might make that would prompt you to return?
- Does your pastor or anyone on the parish staff know you by name?
- Are you in a mixed-religion marriage?
- Do you now belong to another faith community? If so, which one?
- Did you ever really consider yourself to be a member of a Catholic parish community?

A way must be found to elicit honest answers to open-end questions aimed at identifying specific Catholic doctrines or practices that may have caused the break. Often there are misunderstandings of doctrine that require attention. Whether the respondent is male or female should be known along with an assessment of how the respondent regards the status of women in the Church. And, of course, the quality of preaching and the worship environment are important factors in encouraging or discouraging attendance and participation, so what do those who no longer show up think about those factors?

If one has stopped going to Mass, that means he or she is separated from reception of the Eucharist. Hence, the importance of finding a way to reeducate or, perhaps explain for the first time the centrality of the Eucharist to Catholic life.

A skillful exit interviewer will find ways of detecting secular political influences as well as social class considerations that might influence the decision to leave a Catholic worshipping community.

Lay expertise in designing and implementing an exit-interview schedule is needed along with the commitment on the part of parish and diocesan authorities to use it. Whatever imagery applies—sleepwalking into the future, walking with eyes and ears closed to those we want to serve—the Church in America has to face the fact of failure to communicate the good news cheerfully and effectively to a population that is adrift on a sea of materialism and under constant attack from the forces of secularism, not to mention the diabolical powers that are at work in our world.

Creative use of the exit interview may well be the key to discovery of reentry portals as well as finding ways to strengthen the American Catholic worshipping community. It may also identify what needs to be done by way of seminary training or retraining those called to positions of leadership in the parishes. All we have to lose by initiating exit interviews is ignorance. Let the process begin.

59.

Justice, Vengeance, and Saddam Hussein

Justice and vengeance are not interchangeable terms. Yet we often say justice when we mean vengeance and act vengefully in the name of justice. "Bringing them to justice" too often means turning them over to a violent end.

Saddam Hussein "got his," as they say, on the gallows just a few days before history closed the books on the year 2006, a violent one by any measure in the Middle East and other parts of the world. Iraq's Ministry of Justice decided that death by hanging evened the score for the deaths of 148 men and boys, murdered on orders from Hussein in Dujail, Iraq, in 1982. Presumably, Hussein was "getting even" for an earlier assassination attempt on his life in that same town, not to mention the hundreds of thousands of his own countrymen who lost their lives by the will and command of this brutal dictator in torture chambers, in the wars he started with Iran and Kuwait, and in acts of vengeance against his political enemies. Countless lives, not just the 148 for which he was tried, weighed in on his guilty verdict. Saddam Hussein was, by all accounts, an evil man.

Is the world a better place without him? Without Hussein's brutality and callous disregard for life, freedom, and dignity of countless human beings? Yes, certainly. But without Hussein the human being, who might have been contained and controlled by authorities capable of preventing him from harming others? Who can say?

Capital punishment is unjustifiable (notice the word *just* in the middle of that term) if the state can contain and control (all the while attempting to correct) an evil, brutal, murderer who would thus never be able to harm or kill again. Whenever a human being, even one who sins against

God in whose image he or she has been created, is involved, there has to be ray of hope, even for the incorrigible.

When will we ever learn that violence is an unacceptable instrument of social and political change? When will we begin to notice that violence begets violence and that vengeance adds nothing to justice; it simply subtracts from human dignity, the dignity of the vengeful.

We are accustomed to imaging or representing justice symbolically as trays in balance on a scale. We are also used to speaking of justice in a building-trades vocabulary of "on the level," or "upright," and in expressions like "fair and square," "up and up," and "even-handed."

Put hundreds of thousands, more likely millions, of murdered lives on the one tray and then put the executed life of Saddam Hussein on the other. Does that even up anything? Is there more justice in the world as a result? Is that action of execution upright?

Set vengeance aside for a moment as unworthy of us humans, and shift the context from justice to mercy. We all know that the whole human race landed on the downside tray as a result of the sacrificial love of Jesus and the trays were back in balance. Justice was born of mercy. The arithmetic of justice cannot be compared with the arithmetic of mercy.

With the birth, life, death, and resurrection of one man —the God-man—the Sun of Justice rose. "Blessed are the merciful," said Jesus, "for they will receive mercy" (Matt 5:7).

The death by hanging of Saddam Hussein, now long forgotten by most of us, might have been an occasion to read the mercy meter in our own hearts and say a prayer for those most in need of mercy. Perhaps the next public execution, "in the name of justice," will prompt some of us to do just that.